TIMBER FRAMED BUILDINGS EXPLAINED

― **TREVOR YORKE** ―

COUNTRYSIDE BOOKS
NEWBURY BERKSHIRE

First published 2010
© Trevor Yorke 2010
Reprinted 2014, 2016, 2018, 2021, 2025

All rights reserved. No reproduction
permitted without the prior permission
of the publisher:

COUNTRYSIDE BOOKS
3 Catherine Road
Newbury, Berkshire

To view our complete range of books,
please visit us at
www.countrysidebooks.co.uk

ISBN 978 1 84674 220 0

Photographs and illustrations by the author

Designed by Peter Davies, Nautilus Design
Produced through The Letterworks Ltd., Reading
Typeset by KT Designs, St Helens
Printed by The Holywell Press, Oxford

CONTENTS

INTRODUCTION 5

SECTION I

A HISTORY OF TIMBER FRAMED BUILDINGS
7

Chapter 1

DEFINITION AND ORIGINS
8

Chapter 2

MEDIEVAL
1200–1450
13

Chapter 3

TUDOR AND STUART
1450–1700
25

Chapter 4

GEORGIAN AND MODERN
1700–2000
36

SECTION II

Timber Framed Buildings in Detail
44

Chapter 5
The Frame
Posts, Beams and Trusses
45

Chapter 6
The Infill
Wattle and Daub and Roof Coverings
57

Chapter 7
The Fittings
Windows, Doors and Floors
65

Further Information
74

Places to Visit
75

Glossary
77

Index
79

Introduction

History is rarely displayed in such a forthright manner as on a timber framed building. From a distance the contorted structure of bowing beams and leaning posts creates an impression that it has been ravaged by centuries of wear and tear, while countless generations have looked through its delicate leaded windows. On closer inspection the rustic timbers hewn by hands possibly six or seven hundred years ago, the rough chalky panels between them and the creaking stairs and doors fill our senses with antiquity. These historic medieval halls, grand Tudor houses or quaint thatched cottages have long been appreciated; painters and architects have used them as sources of inspiration ever since the English countryside and the Picturesque became influential in art from the early 19th century.

The problem when looking at timber framed buildings today is that after centuries of occupation they have been altered many times over and modern renovation has created forms that are not completely original. The familiar stark black and white timber structure with the main body divided into small rooms with low ceilings would come as a shock to the carpenter who first built it. There are also many more that are hidden behind later walls, as before the Victorian period symmetry and brick were fashionable, it was common to cover up the building's rustic origins. You could be surprised to discover how many timber framed structures you can find behind brick and stone façades if you look down a side alley or under an archway in most of our old towns and villages.

This book sets out to help you understand what these buildings originally looked like, how they changed over the centuries and why they fell from favour. It will help you recognise the details by which they can be dated, understand the methods of construction, and identify those that are hidden from view. Using my own drawings, diagrams and photos it conveys this information in a pictorial form, acting as a layman's introduction to the subject and with suggested places to visit and further reading if you wish to find out more about the regional variations and architectural details of these historic buildings.

The first section explains the background and basic principles of timber framed buildings and then tells the story of how they rose to prominence and then were superseded over the centuries. It concentrates on those structures that are still standing and contains photos in each chapter of examples to be seen today, many of which can be accessed by the public. The second half of the book looks in detail at how they were built, the materials used and the types of fittings that would have originally been inserted into the frame. It explains how the timber was produced, the parts assembled and the finished structure protected from the elements and reveals the reason behind some of the fascinating details you can see when visiting or living in a timber framed building.

Trevor Yorke

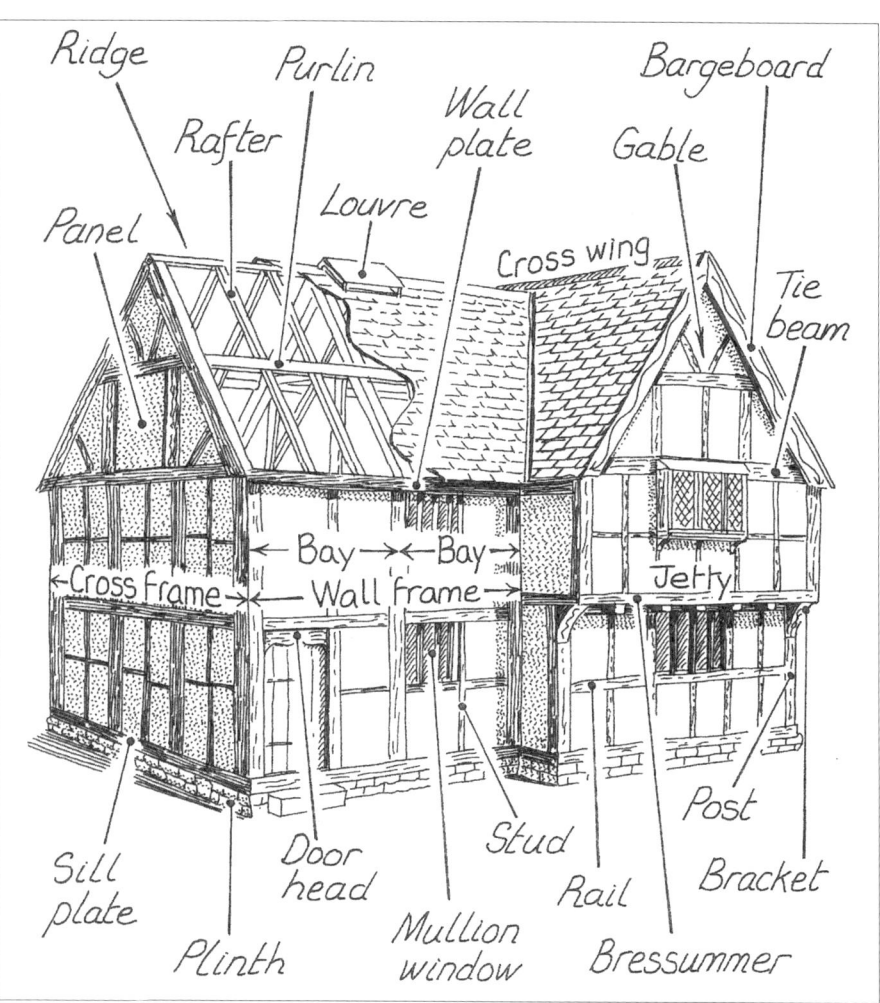

Section I

A History of Timber Framed Buildings

Chapter 1

Definition and Origins

![Little Moreton Hall]

FIG 1.1: LITTLE MORETON HALL, CHESHIRE (NT): *This most famous of timber framed houses was begun in the 15th century. The whole of this picture (the three-storey building) shows the south range, built a century after the north and east range. The projection next to the bridge is the entrance porch and the long row of windows along the upper floor, the long gallery. Outwardly, it appears as a large substantial structure, yet once inside you find it is formed from a ring of thin rectangular boxes arranged around a courtyard.*

Ask most people what a timber framed building looks like and they will describe an old house with black wooden beams, white panels between and a tiled or thatched roof above. This distinctive form,

Definition and Origins

unique to this island, has in the past century been an icon of our countryside, featuring on countless images of rural England and attracting millions of visitors to the finest remaining examples. Before looking at them in detail we first need to put them in context. What date are the earliest buildings, when did they fall from favour and what exactly do we mean by timber framing?

What is a timber framed building?

A timber framed building is one in which a principal framework of vertical and horizontal or inclined beams form the main load-bearing support for the upper floors and roof. The infill between them and any outer cladding of stone, brick, tile or timber is purely to weatherproof the structure and to change its outward appearance to suit the whims of fashion. Each wall of the structure is a separate frame, which was prefabricated before being raised or reconstructed in position and linked together. The individual parts were connected by different joints, each one designed to counter the forces applied to it through its shape and the inclusion of wooden pegs (later buildings used iron bolts and straps).

The carpenter had to select timber of suitable thickness to support the main frame and the additional load imposed

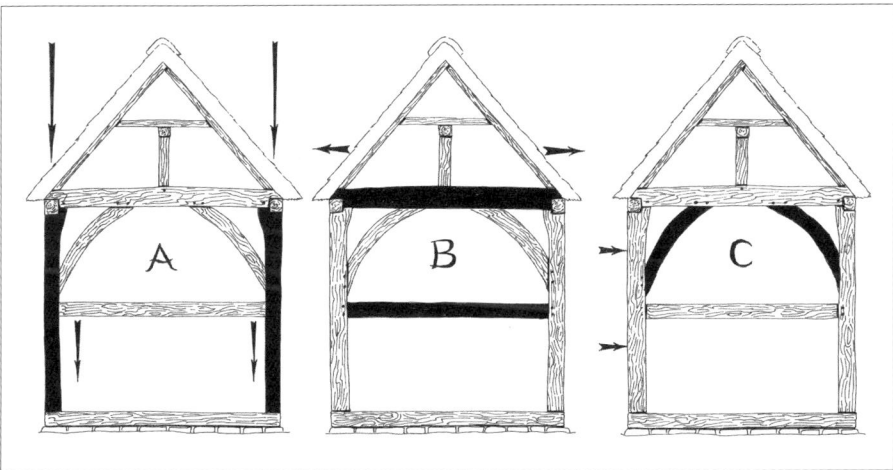

FIG 1.2: *A view through the side of a medieval timber framed house, highlighting in black the elements that are resisting a force applied in the direction of the arrows. In A the posts take the weight applied vertically from the roof covering, rafters and floor, in B the horizontal beams resist the spreading effect of the roof and in C the angled struts stop the whole toppling over in a side wind. In the latter example the timbers are forming a triangle, which is the one geometric shape that cannot be distorted and is key to keeping timber framed buildings rigid.*

upon it from fittings and people, falls of snow on the roof and the weight of the building materials themselves. He also had to account for sideways pressure from wind and movement in the foundations and so inserted diagonal struts and braces to resist these. The breadth of timber, the size of the panels, and the patterns formed in each of these frames are the most distinctive features of the building, seen from the outside, which can help to arrive at an approximate date.

The key problem facing builders in the past was how to hold up the roof and in our wet climate a steep pitched type covered in thatch, stone or clay tiles was the traditional form prior to the Industrial Revolution. If you have ever tried to stand two playing cards up by leaning them against each other on a table you will soon realise that they have to be nearly vertical (like a steeple) before they will stay in place; any angle less than this and their bottom edges simply push outwards and they collapse. In effect this is what a roof is trying to do to the walls of the building below and the structure has to be designed to resist this force and the total weight of the rafters and covering.

In traditional timber framed construction this was achieved by generally using steep pitched roofs (the angle depending on the weight and rain shedding properties of the covering material) and different types of roof truss or arrangement of posts and beams, which hold the rafters up from beneath and tie the bottom edges so they cannot push outwards. Their form varies through time and in different regions. When trying to discover the origins of a building it is these hidden structures in the loft that experts seek to ascertain its original dimensions and form.

Most timber framed buildings prior to the late 17th century were built one main room deep and were rectangular in plan (there was a limit to how big a gap a horizontal beam could cross

FIG 1.3: *Common methods of extending a basic timber framed structure at a later date. The beauty of a framed structure is that these extensions are easily fitted and add to its stability; cross wings at right angles resisted wind pressure applied to the ends of the original building and catslides propped up the main walls to counter the spread of the roof.*

before sagging and breaking). This basic form was subdivided into bays, each one being the space between the principal load-bearing posts (see page 6). Any additional space required could be created by extending this form lengthways, but more often carpenters added wings across the ends or built a lean-to structure along the rear (see Fig 1.3). In larger buildings the structure could have aisles along each side to increase space or have its parts arranged around a courtyard, outwardly appearing as more substantial but still having its individual parts only one room deep (see Fig 1.1).

Why build in timber?

Despite the close proximity of suitable stone and skilled brickmakers, timber framed structures were still the dominant form of building across the country well into the 17th century. This was mainly because these alternative forms were very expensive. There were few permanent quarries, most local ones being opened for just a single major project, and masons tended to congregate around principal cities and the cost of their services were out of the range of even some lords of the manor. Bricks were handmade to order on site, the skills required making them a costly material, that was generally restricted to the eastern and south-east counties until the later Tudor period and was still not common in the west until the 18th century. It was also difficult to move these products any distance, roads were poor and rivers limited in scope, so materials and skilled workmen were generally supplied from the locality,

creating vernacular forms of building. Because reliable sources of wood and the knowledge and tools required to work it were widely available, timber framed structures – usually with roofs covered in equally abundant thatch – were the type that most people lived in until the 17th century and, in some rural areas, beyond.

FIG 1.4: THE ROEBUCK, LEEK, STAFFORDSHIRE: *Legend has it that this pub dating from the 1620s was moved from Shropshire some 40 miles away. Although these prefabricated structures could be disassembled, the transporting of hundreds of heavy beams and posts over this distance is unlikely with such poor roads. It would be easier and more cost effective to build with local materials and methods of construction passed down from father to son and the vast majority of timber framed buildings were of vernacular style.*

When did timber framing first appear?

Man has always used timber in the building of structures since he first started clearing woodland after the last ice age. However, in most prehistoric examples a structural framework with carpentry joints was not used; an Iron Age round house, for instance, had long poles held in position by a timber ring to form a conical roof, which stood upon low walls of stone, clay or posts.

The Romans certainly used timber framed houses even in their towns and cities. New research is showing that earlier calculations of population may have been wrong because archaeologists underestimated the numbers of these buildings as they did not always leave foundations in the ground. During the Saxon period forms of construction from Scandinavia and Northern Europe seem to have been adopted with vertical halved trunks, posts or planks set in trenches to form solid rather than framed walls.

Where the familiar timber framed structure developed from and why is not known, but it is likely that, as the population expanded from the later Saxon period and more woodland was cleared for farming, there were not sufficient large pieces of timber to form solid walls. At some point it was realised that by spacing the posts out and filling the gaps between with more readily available materials, walls could be formed. Horizontal beams would give the wall stability and a sill below some protection against damp, so that by the late 12th century, when our earliest surviving examples were built, a fully developed form of timber framed construction had appeared. This is where our story begins – with medieval houses, barns, guild halls and market houses dating from the late 1100s through to the mid 1400s.

FIG 1.5: GREENSTED CHURCH ESSEX: *A unique timber walled Saxon church made from split logs originally set into the earth. At a later date they were cut back and a timber sill and brick footing was inserted, as seen in this picture. Some of the logs date to the 9th century. A tool that researchers can now use to help date buildings like this is dendrochronology where a core sample taken from a timber creates a barcode effect with the different widths of ring depending on wet and dry years of growth. This is compared against a local catalogue to find a match, which can even pinpoint the time of year the tree was felled!*

CHAPTER 2

Medieval
1200–1450

FIG 2.1: THE BELL, WALTHAM ST LAWRENCE, BERKSHIRE: *Surviving medieval timber framed buildings are generally few but those dating from the 15th century are the most common. One distinctive type is known as Wealden (from the Weald of Kent and Sussex where they originated) and as in this example they have jettied first floors either side of a central recess, behind which was an open hall.*

The 250 years covered in this chapter span a part of the medieval period in which there were great fluctuations in the fortunes of individuals. A booming population in the 13th century was savagely cut down by nearly half after famine and plague in the 14th. Most people were tied into the feudal system in 1200, born in a community where they would remain all their lives with little opportunity to better themselves. By

1450 this rigid social order had broken down and the ambitious could cross social barriers and a new class of merchants and yeoman farmers appeared.

The earliest timber framed buildings that survive generally belonged to the aristocracy or those connected to the Church and abbeys, but by the end of this period a broader spectrum can be found, in many cases financed by this new class of wealthy families. Urban shops, farmhouses, guild halls, market buildings, and in some areas even churches, were erected from posts and beams while the rich built themselves more palatial fortified homes and stout manor houses.

However, these represent but a tiny proportion of the buildings that would have stood, those that housed the majority of the population have long since gone. Built from less substantial timbers with wattle, clay or rubble walls, they were designed to last only a generation or two and any that survived longer were swept aside during the great rebuilding of Britain through the 17th and 18th centuries. What you see today is the medieval equivalent of your modern High Street with a sprinkling of Chelsea and Alderley Edge!

Timber framed houses

Most medieval houses had one principal open room; in the largest buildings it was a hall, a grand space where the owner could eat, drink, manage his estate, administer justice and entertain guests. It could be a freestanding building or the central part of a house and would appear as a rectangular planned structure with a steep pitched roof, typically with a main entrance at one end and a large window at the other. Inside would have been a huge open space with its layout carefully reflecting the social status of the occupants, a plan which varies little across the country.

If you imagine walking in through the main entrance, the first part you would see would be a dark passage screened off from the hall to keep draughts out (the screens or cross passage) with two or three doors on your right leading to the service rooms. Turn left through the gaps in the wooden panelled screen and you would have entered a space similar to the nave of a church, full of noise, colour and smoke. The fire would be in the middle

FIG 2.2: *The vast majority of people worked in the country and lived in homes with just one principal room, some having one end of a long house reserved for livestock. These simple structures, as in the example above, may have been rebuilt every 25–50 years.*

MEDIEVAL

FIG 2.3: *A medieval hall as it may have originally appeared, with labels of some of the key parts. The emphasis was focused upon the upper end where the owner sat (opposite the entrance,) and the largest windows, the finest decoration and even the best face of any exposed truss in the ceiling would be directed towards this part. Most timber framed examples were divided into two unequal bays with a load-bearing frame or truss exposed in the centre.*

or tucked up in a corner beneath a large hood while long tables and benches would run up its length, with those of lower social status in this end of the room and those of greater importance at the top. In this upper end would be the owner's table, raised upon a low platform called a dais, with large windows illuminating it and a canopy or decorated beam above emphasising its superiority. In surviving unaltered examples today you can still see the strict structure of medieval society reflected in its plan and decoration.

Medieval towns and cities, apart from London, were very small, with nearly all housing concentrated around a market place and the main roads leading from it. Much of it would have stood at the head of thin strips of land known as burgage plots, these distinctive divisions remaining in many urban centres today. The houses themselves were very different in layout

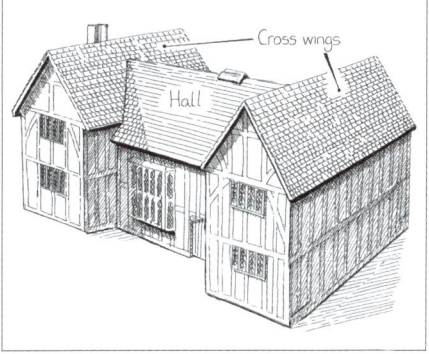

FIG 2.4: *By the later medieval period local lords sought greater privacy from their staff so existing halls were extended and new ones built with cross wings at one or both ends, as in the above example. These provided private chambers for the owner in the wing behind the dais with a small door leading off to one side into a two-storey structure (today often referred to as a solar). Larger service rooms and further accommodation could be added at the other end. It is important to remember that in larger houses this would have been one of several buildings, such as a kitchen, guest rooms and stables, loosely arranged around a walled enclosure with a gateway over the entrance. Most of these would have been timber framed even if the hall was in stone.*

FIG 2.5: *Cut away views of two types of urban house, one with a narrow frontage (top) and the gable facing out, the other on a wider plot with the roof running left to right and facing the road (bottom). The top example has a small shop at the front with lift-up shutters to secure the property when closed. Many of these narrow fronted plots were laid out when new markets were established or towns redeveloped in the 12th and 13th centuries. Their originally regular layout can be hard to see at first because the old divisions have broken down, plots have merged and buildings have been rebuilt.*

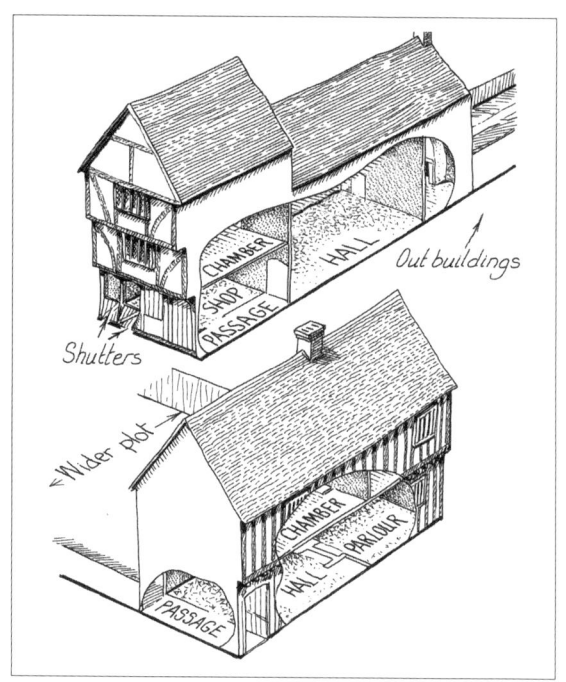

from those in the country, and were shaped to make the most of their narrow frontage. They often had small shops at the front, which they could rent out, and a passage down the side leading to the hall behind, with chambers above and a line of service and storage buildings further down the rear. The façade onto the street was the one opportunity for display and many were highly decorative and colourful. However, their biggest problem was fire, and although some towns and cities had regulations to insert stone walls between timber framed houses to reduce its spread (some survive today), many houses were destroyed by regular conflagrations over the centuries.

FIG 2.6: *A large medieval house as it may have originally appeared, with heavy timbers, large panels and long braces.*

Medieval

Types of structure

Although some of the earliest surviving examples used long pieces of regular cross section timber (uniform scantling) most medieval examples that survive are notable for heavy and thick principal posts and beams. The panels between these tend to be large, some without any intermediate studs forming a division. The inclusion of very long, slightly curving braces on the façade is very distinctive of this period, and there is generally a greater use of bowed and irregular timbers in the construction than in later centuries. In the country these braces tend to rise up from the post to the wall plate but on urban façades they are usually found running from the top corner down to the middle, with a window set between.

The form of the frame varied depending upon the region and the scale of the building. The limitation in the length of the tie beam across the structure and the weight and outward pressure of the roof when spanning a large space like a hall or barn had, since the late Saxon period, resulted in the development of aisled buildings. In effect these were a box-shaped middle section with lean-to structures running along either side, but all under one large continuous roof, so inside they have two lines of posts dividing the central nave from the aisles.

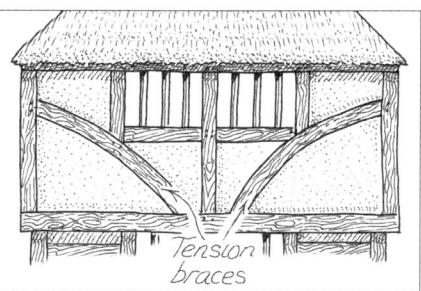

FIG 2.7: *This form of bracing was popular on urban façades across the country but is called Kentish framing after its popularity in that county and much of the South-East and East Anglia. The two braces are in part holding up the centre of the beam to resist its tendency to sag, hence they are in tension although at the same time they form triangles, giving the frame stability from sideways movement.*

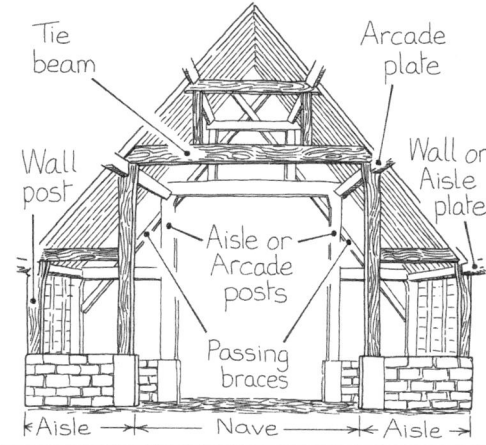

FIG 2.8: *A cut away view through the middle of an aisled barn, showing the main parts of the frame. The aisles in effect buttress the main section while the aisle posts take most of the vertical load from the huge roof and transfer it to the ground, often via a stone column. The arrangement above the tie beam varies greatly and passing braces running diagonally across add extra stability.*

These can be found dating from throughout this period and later in barns where the internal divisions did not restrict its use. In the halls and other large buildings they fell from favour during the 14th century as the posts and tie beams obstructed the space and carpenters came up with alternative methods of supporting the roof. The most elaborate was the hammer beam, which in effect had the central section of the horizontal tie removed and its ends jointed to a short vertical post running up to the collar and an arched brace supporting it from below. This was popular where there was an impressive pointed arch window in the end wall, the view of which would have been blocked by the tie beam, and hence these are most common in churches and the finest stone halls. Another more common solution was to push the tie beam up, in effect making it a collar, and then use two large arched braces below to give support (see Fig 2.9).

Most halls, secular buildings and smaller houses in the east, south and occasionally the finest examples in the north and west were built with a square

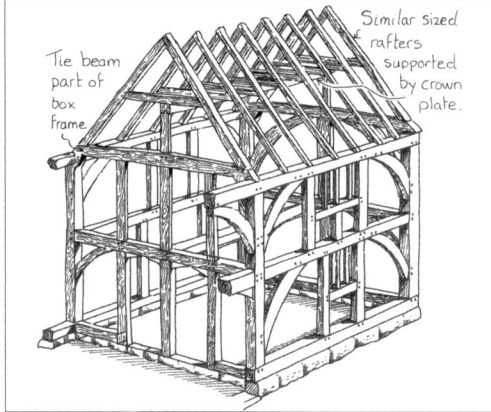

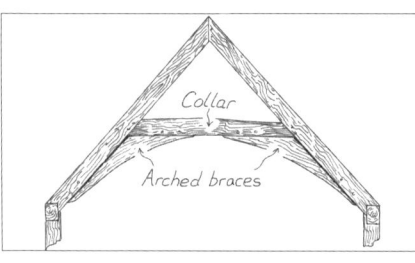

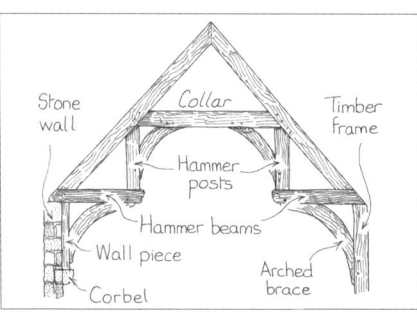

FIG 2.9: *An arched braced collar roof (top) and hammer beam roof (below).*

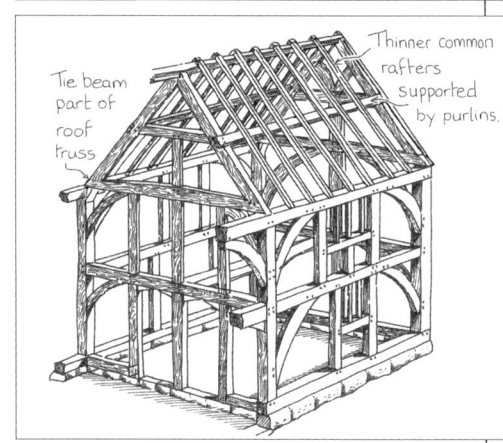

FIG 2.10: *A box framed building (top) and a post and truss type (below).*

frame. There are two distinct forms of these that can be found in this period and later (see Fig 2.10). The first, known as post and truss, had a self supporting truss formed by a tie beam and principal rafters fixed to the top of the vertical wall posts with common rafters between supported on purlins. The second, referred to as box framing, had the wall posts and tie beams making a box, with regular sized rafters above not forming part of the main structure (crown post roofs are this type). These differences are not always obvious from the exterior and the two forms are often referred to just as 'box framed'.

Crucks framing was the dominant form in the north and west of the country and in the highland areas of the Midlands and south-west from around 1200 through to the mid 1500s. Its load-bearing element was a pair of slightly bent beams (usually one trunk cut down the middle to form matching pairs) with their bases set apart to the width of the house and their tops joined together to form a series of triangular supports down the length of the structure. These were held in place by longitudinal timbers, with the front and rear wall just vertical frames adding rigidity and keeping the weather out. The crucks blades, as the main timbers are referred to, are often only visible in part at the end walls so from the front the building may seem similar to box types.

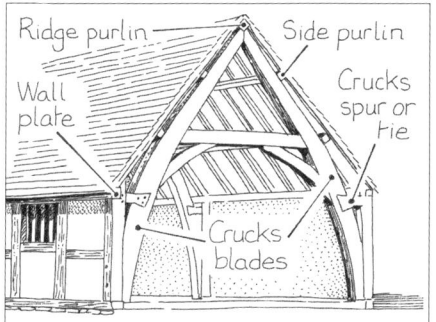

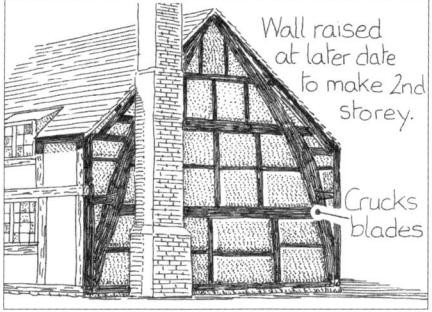

FIG 2.11: *A cut-away view of a crucks framed house as it may originally have appeared, and a view below of the same one today from the outside. An extra storey and chimney have been added but the crucks blades are still visible. It is worth looking down the side of buildings to see if you can spot even just a part of these distinctive curving timbers.*

Regional details

In East Anglia, a rich and important area in this period, the finest box framed houses had close set vertical timbers 1–2 ft apart, running the full height of each storey in a form known as close studding. The arched braces, which are essential to keep these houses rigid, were often set behind these so are not usually visible from the exterior. This excessive use of timber was a display of the owner's wealth,

FIG 2.12: *Close studded buildings from Suffolk dating from the 15th century (the windows are later insertions).*

longitudinal support from purlins, a horizontal timber fixed to the principal pair, which held up the common rafters between them. These could be used on crucks frame and post and truss structures, the latter usually confined to the finest buildings, where a pair of principal rafters had only a collar between them and arched braces below (see Fig 2.10, lower drawing).

In the northern counties, a sturdy but tends to be restricted to this area and neighbouring counties in this period.

In the box framed houses – these were dominant in East Anglia and the South East – the roof was supported on rafters, which in the earliest and simplest examples were only stopped from toppling over by the thin strips of wood nailed horizontally along them (laths) onto which the covering was fixed. An improvement to this was the crown post roof in which a central post rose up from the tie beam to support a crown plate that ran the length of the house; off this were fixed horizontal collars to hold up each rafter (Fig 2.13 top). This rather long-winded method was popular in these regions throughout the medieval period but quickly fell from favour in the early 16th century.

In the western half of the country the rafters of larger houses usually gained

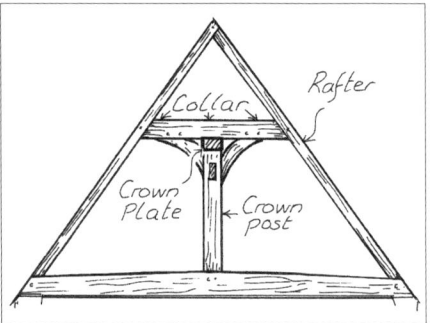

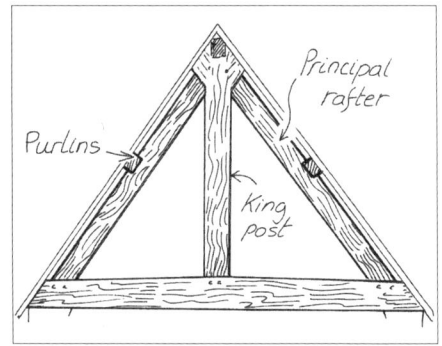

FIG 2.13: *A crown post roof (top) with arched braces emerging from the top of the post to make a 'crown-like' form. The king post (below) forms a rigid truss that supported slender purlins cut into the upper surface of the principal rafters.*

MEDIEVAL

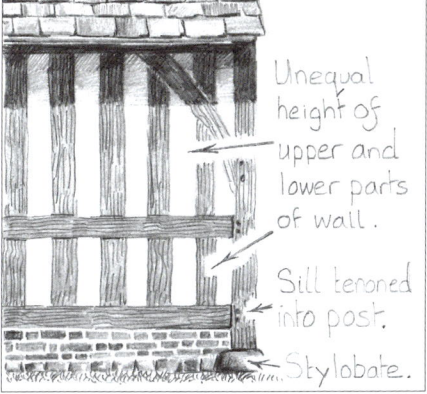

FIG 2.14: *On the Yorkshire side of the Pennines a distinctive form of hall was popular in the late medieval period. They had close studded walls but unlike their East Anglian counterparts the two storeys were of unequal height. The main posts also rested directly upon a pad stone (stylobate), with the sill plate raised upon a low wall and joined into the side of the post. Most of these were later covered by stone walls so are not clear at first, except in restored examples.*

roofs with just collars and purlins; there are also aisles but often just along one side with the other keeping the large window to illuminate the principal room.

STILL OUT THERE:

FIG 2.15: MARTON, CHESHIRE: *Timber framing was often used for building parts of a church, like a new porch, bell tower or roof, with some of the finest medieval carpentry reserved for elaborate trusses and decoration on the ceiling within. However, in some areas, such as Cheshire, complete churches were constructed with timber frames. St James and St Paul's church here at Marton has an aisled body (see Fig 2.8) all under one roof and a tower with lean-to structures around its exposed sides. Dating from the late 14th century, it is amongst the oldest of its type in Europe.*

central post running up from the tie beam to a ridge plate or purlin, with the principal rafters joined into it at the top, was common in large buildings. These king post roofs were crude, undecorated but effective; however, some crown post types were also used, perhaps because this form from the prosperous south and east was seen as a sign of wealth. In the lowland areas of Yorkshire some important buildings display a combination of features from neighbouring areas. They can have two close studded walls of equal height but

FIG 2.16: *Sometimes the type of timber framed structure underneath later render and brickwork can be identified by looking down the sides of buildings. These two end gables from York have their crown post roofs on display with angled struts to each side and the crown plate protruding from the left hand post (see Fig 2.13 top).*

FIG 2.18: WEALD AND DOWNLAND MUSEUM, SINGLETON, WEST SUSSEX: *Probably the finest display of timber framed buildings in their original form can be seen at this outstanding open museum. The Wealden type building above would have been a home for a prosperous farmer and has been shown with its original open mullioned windows. Note also the Kentish framing, which was popular in the rural south-east of England.*

FIG 2.17: *Inns and pubs are amongst the oldest timber framed buildings that you can find today. Some, as in this example from Ludlow, still have their distinctive narrow courtyards at the rear, with in this case a long wing dating from the 15th century on the right-hand side.*

FIG 2.19: TEWKESBURY, GLOUCESTERSHIRE: *The Abbey Row cottages shown above were built as shops in around 1450 by the local monastery as a commercial enterprise. The shutters over the windows hinged down to form counters. No 45, the Merchant's House, has been restored as a museum.*

MEDIEVAL

FIG 2.20: AVONCRAFT MUSEUM OF HISTORIC BUILDINGS, BROMSGROVE, WORCESTERSHIRE: *This 15th-century hall with a two-storey cross wing is one of the finest exhibits at this excellent open museum, which contains a wide range of buildings, from medieval shops to 1950s prefabs. Note the tiled opening on the roof to vent the fire.*

FIG 2.21: LEIGH COURT BARN, WORCESTESHIRE (EH): *This crucks framed barn is the largest example of its type in Britain (see Fig 2.11). As with many of the finest medieval barns, it was built to store produce collected off the estates of important abbeys, in this case Pershore Abbey (they were not for holding goods paid as a tithe although they are often referred to as such). The diagonal timbers on the underside of the roof are wind braces.*

FIG 2.22: THE KING'S HEAD, SHREWSBURY: *This outstanding medieval building with its distinctive large panels and thick timbers was built in around 1400, although the roof and windows have been changed since. The upper two storeys are jettied out, a new feature that would soon become fashionable on urban properties as during the later 15th century significant changes to the structure of timber framed buildings began to take place. Some types that were previously only found in one area spread out across the country while other forms fell from favour. Why these changes occurred and how they transformed buildings is explained in the following chapter.*

Timber Framed Buildings Explained

FIG 2.23: WEOBLEY, HEREFORDSHIRE: *The four views on this page are all from this incredible village, which is dominated by medieval timber framed houses. The above example at the rear of the Red Lion has a crucks frame clearly displayed in the end gable wall.*

FIG 2.25: *A characteristic Wealden style building (one half of the Unicorn Hotel) dating from the 14th century. As with the others on this page it has substantial timbers especially on the angles and large plain panels.*

FIG 2.24: *Occasionally the whole lower storey is built of stone and the timber framed structure sits on top. This 14th-century example has angled braces either side of the windows, the ones in the foreground with concave cuts in the lower edge, called cusps. The windows and porch are late 18th-century additions.*

FIG 2.26: *This 14th-century building has braces forming Gothic pointed arches on the end gable and the heads of old windows along the side just under the eaves.*

Chapter 3

 # *Tudor and Stuart*
—— *1450–1700* ——

FIG 3.1: THE SHAMBLES, YORK: *This medieval street where butchers used to occupy the shops is an incredible survivor, giving a unique glimpse of how urban centres would have appeared in the Tudor period. Towering buildings with jetties stepping out to block the light, while below the noise and smell from the shops must have been potent. Jetties had been used in late medieval houses, as with some in this view, but it was in the 16th century that it became the must-have status symbol.*

After more than a century of regular outbreaks of plague, which had hampered the population, the 16th century was witness to a turn around in fortunes as numbers increased and business opportunities meant wealth became more dispersed. The Dissolution of the Monasteries in the 1530s placed their large estates into secular hands, with the new landlords waiting to see if Henry VIII's separation from the

Catholic Church became a permanent move, before building new mansions and manor houses for themselves later in the 16th century. These new homes were now influenced by Classical architecture from the Continent, at first just applied decoration but by the following century embodying the whole approach to the design of the structure, with symmetrical façades and large vertical windows. Important buildings became outward looking, proud statements of the owner's fortune and good taste, and by the time of the Restoration in 1660 they were almost exclusively using brick and stone.

In the country, medieval communal agriculture based in large open fields was being replaced by individual yeoman farmers employing workers on newly enclosed land, and building themselves stout new farmhouses.

Those further down the social ladder who benefited from these changes also erected new, more permanent homes, still small by later standards but of a form that would last hundreds of years rather than just a generation. In the towns and cities, merchants, traders, innkeepers and professionals built new houses and businesses, towering over the narrow streets, while the more benevolent endowed new schools, almshouses and communal buildings. Although some were timber framed, the ever-present threat of fire made fashionable brick and stone desirable, especially after the Great Fire of London in 1666 when regulations banning timber and thatch were enforced more vigorously. It is likely that many of the timber framed buildings you see today date from the late 16th and early 17th century, in an

FIG 3.2: *With the breakdown of the old feudal system ambitious families, who in previous generations had been peasants scratching a living from strips on communal fields, could seize the opportunity and establish themselves as yeoman farmers with their own enclosed land and a fine farmhouse built in the village. This example has a brick chimney built up through the centre of the timber framed house, an important feature that enabled the owner to change the interior layout at the same time as displaying his success.*

Tudor and Stuart

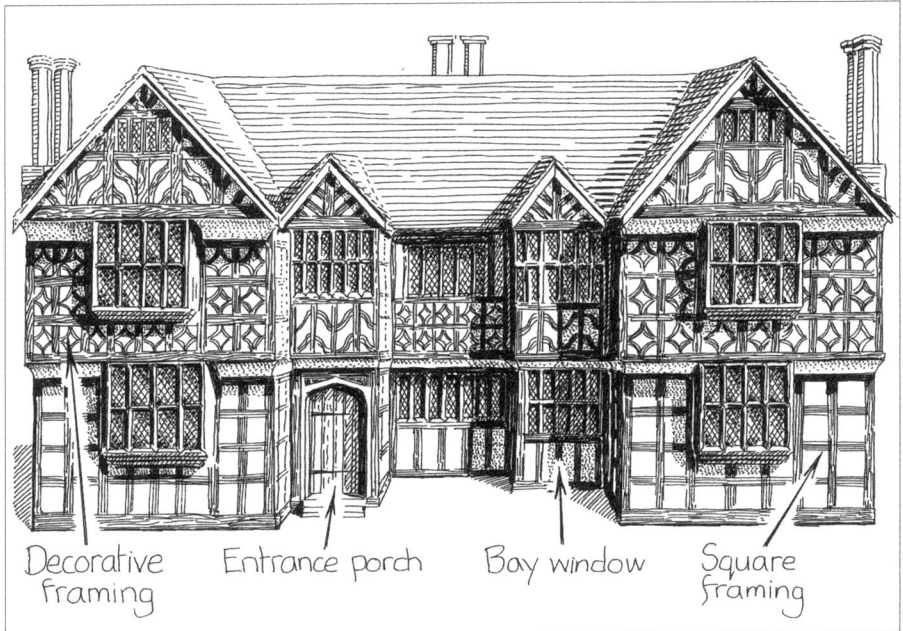

Decorative framing — Entrance porch — Bay window — Square framing

FIG 3.3: *In the largest houses tall porches with little rooms above the doorway and glazed bay windows that stepped out from the line of the wall were a popular addition to older properties. With upper floors being inserted, an external stair turret was often included on new houses or was added to older ones.*

age that saw a gradual replacing of old with new and has been termed 'the Great Rebuilding' by modern historians.

Timber framed houses

Most of the new permanent houses erected in this period remained rectangular structures, one principal room deep, although it became common later to extend this by adding a lean-to extension along the rear (catslide) so they appear more substantial. A few timber framed structures were built double piled (two rooms deep), mainly in the late 17th century, but by this time those who could afford this were more often using brick or stone. These new rural houses were shaped by the position of the latest must-have feature, the chimney and fireplace. Although they had been fitted on some late medieval buildings and were a fashion statement for the Tudor rich, it was not until the late 16th century that they began to be found further down the social ladder.

In the east and south of the country it was common for a stout brick chimneystack to be in the middle of the

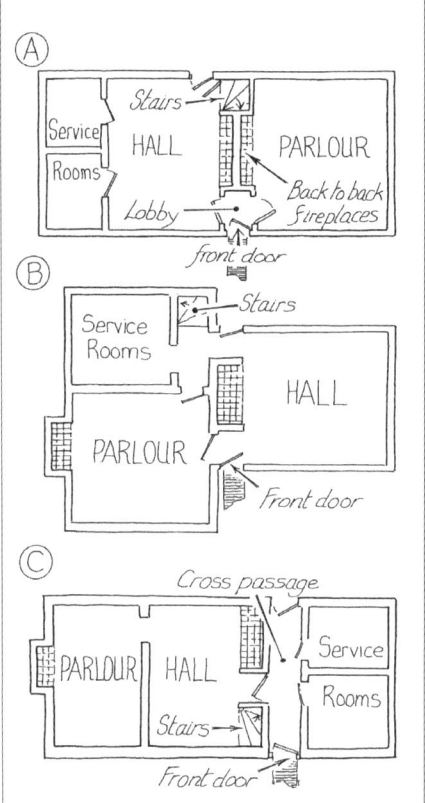

FIG 3.5: *A lobby entrance house for a yeoman farmer, with two ground floor rooms heated by central fireplaces. The hall was where food preparation, cooking and day-to-day work took place and the parlour was for relaxing and meeting people (from 'parler' the French verb 'to speak').*

FIG 3.4: *Three plans of houses and the position of their chimneys marked by the grid symbol. (A) is a lobby entrance type, (B) a 'T'-shaped farmhouse popular in the Midlands and (C) a cross passage cottage common in the north and west of the country.*

house with a short entrance lobby in front of it. In the highland regions cross passages remained common, even in simple cottages, and the fireplace was usually backing onto it in the middle of the main room or was built on the external wall. The latter was a common position for the chimneystack where it was added to an existing timber framed house at a later date, usually on an end gable wall.

The advantage of the chimney, apart from creating a more efficient fire, was that the smoke was channelled so an upper floor could be inserted and sleeping chambers provided upstairs. This division echoes the social changes that had taken place during the 16th century as the lesser gentry, merchants and farmers sought to imitate the aristocracy and no longer wished to live and sleep in a communal hall but

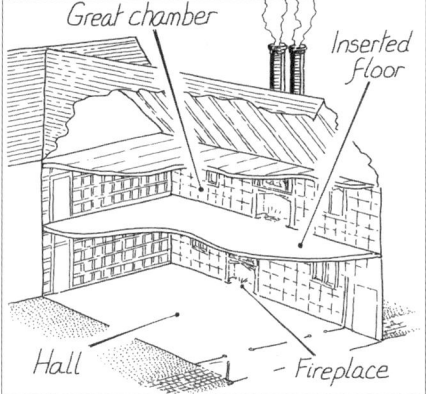

sought privacy, with a separate room set aside for socialising.

Urban houses had chimneys added in a similar way to free the inside so upper floors could be inserted; however, further expansion on their restrictive narrow plots meant that they usually expanded upwards, either adding onto

FIG 3.6: *A medieval hall (top) and the same room in Tudor times (bottom). Already in the later medieval period the wealthy had sought privacy from the open communal hall with private chambers added on in cross wings; in the 16th century it became the fashion to insert floors above it to create a great chamber, which became their personal dining and meeting room, with the hall below relegated in importance. This was only possible because chimneys controlled the smoke from the fires and enabled them to be fitted in upstairs rooms.*

FIG 3.7: *Jetties were the must-have feature of 16th-century urban buildings although they are more rare in rural areas, often just featuring on a wing or one face of a large house. Some had the ends of the joists exposed (top), others had them covered behind a decorative panel (bottom) or plastered coving.*

existing structures or building three or four storey structures from scratch. These featured jetties, the short extension of the joists by a foot or two to project the floor above, as in the distinctive scene in Fig 3.1. On wider sites, or where someone had bought out a plot or two next door, a larger building running lengthways onto the street (see Fig 2.5) gave the opportunity for a continuous jetty to be fitted along the whole façade.

These buildings also gave the owner the chance to display another innovation of the age – glass. It had been used in the finest houses and churches previously but most had used internal shutters or oiled cloth to keep out the draughts. From the 16th century, glass became widely available and the small panes set in diamond-shaped lead frames (cames) and wooden surrounds, creating huge long stretches across the whole façade or elaborate projecting windows, were a potent statement often used to maximum effect on inns, halls and the houses of the rich (see also Chapter 7).

Types of structure

Timber framed buildings of the 16th and 17th century are characterised by their use of more regular and straight timber, which is generally thinner and

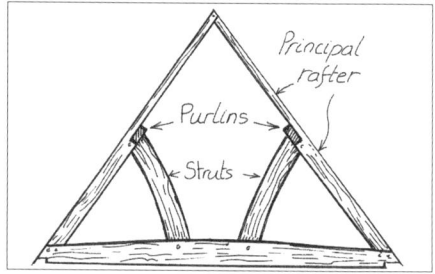

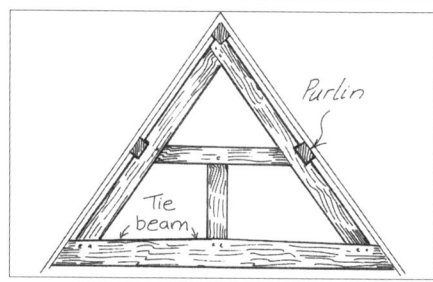

FIG 3.8: *An urban house showing the main innovations of the age: glass in windows and jettied upper floors. Many still had the gable end facing the street due to the limited space but others bought up neighbouring land and built imposing structures with continuous jetties and rows of windows.*

FIG 3.9: *Clasped purlin roof (top) and one with large principal rafters and trenched purlins (bottom). On wider spans additional struts and angle braces could be added for support.*

shorter than that used on medieval structures. This is very evident on angle braces, which rather than being long and curved tended now to be straight and tucked up into a corner. A shortage of good timber certainly affected some places due to demand from early industry and shipbuilding, but the widespread loss of the best oak for sea-going vessels was not a major influence until the growth of trade and the merchant fleet in the 18th century. It may be just that the demands of fashion determined this change or that the shorter, straighter timber formed a more suitable framework for the decorative styles that became distinctive of this age. The panels between the posts also became smaller, either regular shaped square or rectangles, with decorative pieces inserted dependent on region and wealth.

Box framed and post and truss structures became the standard forms as crucks frames fell from favour in the north and west during the 16th century. Trusses within the roof also changed in this period, although the king post remained popular in the north. Crown posts, which had been widespread in the finest houses in the south and east, were superseded by ones with a purlin

FIG 3.10: *It was common for cottages in the late 16th and 17th century to have just a half height upper storey, so to avoid the tie beam running through the middle of this space it was cut in the middle and joined to a vertical beam. Sling braces running diagonally down from the principal rafter to the wall post was a popular solution in the south and east of the country.*

FIG 3.11: *Close studding was used as much as possible by the gentry and farmers, and also upon the finest public buildings. When it was used in the northern and western areas it was common for a middle rail to be inserted, as in the upper floor of this example.*

fitted between the joint of the collar and principal rafter (clasped purlin roofs). These rafters tended to be similar in size to the common ones between so the laths could be nailed level across their upper surfaces. Another solution was the butt purlin where shorter lengths were joined into the sides of principal rafters (butting up to them), forming continuous straight lines in medieval examples but usually staggered so the joints didn't clash on ones from this period. In areas where crucks framing had dominated, roofs with large principal rafters and trenched purlins became the norm.

Regional details

Close studding, which had been a popular form of walling in high class buildings in East Anglia from the 15th century, spread over the south and east and into most urban areas as the style that best displayed the owner's wealth. The more vertical studs you had (some could be as close as a foot apart), the richer you were, simply based upon the extra cost of materials and fitting. Some who could not afford that might simply insert a thin plank between posts or even paint one on the plaster to simulate the effect. However, as with most expensive treatments for a façade, the effect was not continued down the side and rear if they were out of view; here regular square panels, perhaps two

FIG 3.12: *Square panels: Unlike medieval panels, which were large and irregular, those on Tudor and Stuart buildings tended to be of uniform size, approximately 2–3 ft , and are arranged in regular rows.*

FIG 3.13: *Decorative framing: These designs were made by inserting straight and curved pieces into the standard square panels, usually only on a prominent façade. They reflect the Elizabethan and Jacobean love of pattern and can be found in towns and cities across the Midlands, West and North but especially in Shropshire, Cheshire and Lancashire.*

to three feet across, were used and filled with wattle and daub.

This square framing, having originated in Gloucestershire, Herefordshire and Shropshire in the mid 15th century, became a common form for the whole house in many rural areas, from Sussex and Surrey and up into the Midlands and over much of the west and north of England during this period. It was always seen as the poor relation of close studding and even in these parts owners might try and squeeze a row of tightly packed vertical studs along the ground floor as a show of ambition.

In some western and northern counties, especially Cheshire and Lancashire, this square framework could be further enhanced with the insertion of carved pieces of wood to form decorative panels. From the late 16th to mid 17th century the finest houses in this region could have fleur-de-lys, quadrants, stars and herringbone patterns covering their main façades in bold and vibrant displays of wealth.

STILL OUT THERE:

FIG 3.14: LAVENHAM GUILD HALL, SUFFOLK: *Few villages possess the wealth of timber framed buildings that can be found in Lavenham, reflecting its former glory during the peak of the cloth trade in the 15th and 16th centuries. Guilds protecting traders' interests became important bodies in the late medieval period, as reflected in this impressive close studded hall dating from the 1530s. The exterior has been limewashed over, as many buildings probably were.*

FIG 3.15: GREENLAND FISHERY HOUSE, KING'S LYNN: *The last major timber framed house built in the town was for the merchant John Atkin. It was constructed from 1605–8 and had brick nogging between the close studded timbers. A hall ran along the upper floor in this view, originally with small mullion windows under the moulded course (one survives far left) but these were replaced by the larger projecting ones in the late 17th century. King's Lynn has many timber framed buildings with old warehouses behind dating as far back as the 14th century.*

FIG 3.16: ABBOT'S HOUSE, SHREWSBURY: *An imposing building, which was built with shops as an investment by the Abbot, dating from the 1450s, with jetties along both sides.*

FIG 3.18: FORD GREEN HALL, STOKE-ON-TRENT: *Originally a 'T' shaped farmhouse dating from around 1600 onto which was added the porch on the right twenty years later and then a brick wing (far right) in the 18th century. The horizontal rails running through the middle of the vertical close studs on the lower storey and the decorative framing above a row of flat balusters is characteristic of the north and west of England.*

FIG 3.17: THE FEATHERS HOTEL, LUDLOW: *Extravagant decorated framing dates from the re-fronting of an existing building in 1619 (the round arched carving in the gables is typical of Jacobean work). The deeper bay window on the left was originally the porch but the front door was moved and the balcony added in 1840.*

FIG 3.19: THE CROWN HOTEL, NANTWICH, CHESHIRE: *A major fire devastated this town in 1583 and many buildings like this imposing hotel were rebuilt soon after. The continuous jetty with the upper storey filled with glass is typical of the age.*

FIG 3.20: STOKESAY CASTLE GATEHOUSE, SHROPSHIRE (EH): Many country houses in the 15th and 16th centuries were still set within a walled enclosure with new gatehouses built across the entrance to provide accommodation and impress guests. This famous example dates from around 1640.

FIG 3.21: LITTLE MORETON HALL, CHESHIRE (NT): The wealthy's desire to show off their superiority was most visibly displayed in the excessive use of glass, as here in bay windows dating from 1559.

FIG 3.22: BESSIE SURTEES HOUSE, NEWCASTLE UPON TYNE (EH): This huge towering structure is one of a pair of merchant's houses, five storeys high with shallow jetties and continuous rows of windows. The façade today has a rendered finish, including the ends of the joists, and the windows have Classical columns between them. By the late 17th century timber framing seemed out of date compared with the new Classical-inspired buildings with symmetrical brick and stone fronts. In the following chapter we will see how owners tried to update their old houses and why these rustic structures later came back into fashion.

CHAPTER 4

Georgian and Modern
1700–2000

FIG 4.1: *Timber framing came back into fashion in the late 19th century either as decorative cladding or part of the structure, usually above a stone or brick lower storey as in this example by Richard Norman Shaw in Leek, Staffordshire.*

Timber framing as the principal form of building construction for the previous five hundred years began to decline rapidly from around the time of the Restoration of the Monarchy in 1660. There were a number of changes that made brick and stone more suitable and cost effective

GEORGIAN AND MODERN

materials, so that by the 18th century the work of the carpenter was restricted to the internal structure or the poorest quality housing. Fire was one of the main reasons for this; although it had ravaged most towns and villages at some time in the past, the Great Fire of London of 1666 was of such a scale that new building regulations were passed banning the use of timber framed and thatched houses in the city. These had been introduced in many urban areas before but now others began to follow suit, new rules were introduced and existing ones more vigorously enforced.

At the same time, brick production became more widespread and permanent brickworks were established, making bricks cheaper and easier to supply. Local quarries, which had often been opened for single projects, now became full time and the masons to work the stone moved into these areas, making it a cost effective alternative for quality houses and buildings. Not only were these materials fireproof but they were also fashionable and better suited to the refined and symmetrical Classical façades that those with money now desired. Another problem was the increasing shortage of quality timber as demand from industries like iron smelting and shipbuilding reduced the amount of oak available to builders in certain areas, a situation that became widespread in the late 18th century.

For those who could not afford to build from scratch with these new materials, there was an alternative for their now out of date building. In the 18th century it became common practice to encase the timber frame in stone or brick or clad it with weatherboarding or render. This enabled the owner to create a Classical façade with the latest sash windows, an important consideration for businesses along the new turnpike roads for whom the most up to date building was essential for attracting the better class of customer.

For the next hundred and fifty years Classical and Gothic forms in brick and

FIG 4.2: *To help restrict the spread of fire some city authorities forced owners to erect stone or brick walls between timber framed properties, some of which can still be found today.*

the speculative builders who applied these as decorative forms to standard terraces, semis and detached houses as they sought to create a village appearance within the town and city. Although the aftermath of the Second World War saw a rejection of these mock façades, due to shortage of materials as much as taste, the style returned again in the late 20th century as we continue to this day our obsession with a mystical but comforting English rural past.

FIG 4.3: *Many buildings along turnpike roads refaced their timber framed structures with fashionable stone, brick or rendered façades, as in this example from Midhurst, Sussex. A look down the side or at the rear can be most revealing.*

stone dominated all forms of building, until in the second half of the 19th century a new generation of architects sought inspiration from old farm and manor houses and created new styles that included timber framed elements (usually just cladding). Some, in response to the overbearing effects of industry, took this a stage further and established Arts and Crafts groups; architects within these used traditional handmade techniques and vernacular materials to build houses that sometimes can be hard to differentiate from the original timber framed buildings. Their outstanding quality, however, made them expensive and in the first half of the 20th century it was

FIG 4.4: *An Arts and Craft style house, designed in the 1890s, capturing the essence of timber framed buildings with its asymmetrical façade, decorative framing and jetties but mounted upon a stone base with fashionable features like balconies, long rows of short mullion windows and low slung roofs.*

Timber framed housing

Despite the adoption of solid brick and stone to form the main load-bearing walls in most buildings from the late 17th century, there was still an important role for the carpenter. Within these structures, dividing walls, floors and roofs continued to be timber framed and as houses were now usually double piled (two rooms deep) his skills were tested especially with the design of trusses required to span these greater distances. He also had softwoods to work with; imported pine from the Baltic could be of good quality and gave him longer, straighter lengths than were available from indigenous sources. The mass production of iron meant that nails, straps and specialised fittings were cheaper and replaced wooden pegs and carpentry joints in holding the frames together.

Timber framed houses were still built at the bottom end of the market. Rural cottages, especially in poor areas or those where brick and stone were yet to become cheap enough, were erected using thin pieces of timber (not always oak), small square panels and long, slender and straight braces. In some areas like the South East, timber framed houses were built and covered in weatherboarding as part of the original design; in other cases these horizontal timbers or hanging tiles were applied to older structures to bring them up to date or extend their life. In the South West timber frames set

FIG 4.5: *Timber framed houses from the late 17th and 18th centuries tended to use thinner pieces of wood and many were originally or later covered by weatherboarding, brick or tile, as in these examples.*

FIG 4.6: *Weatherboarding was used from the late medieval period in East Anglia to protect buildings from the weather or from the sea and wind along the coast. In the 18th century imported soft wood was used more widely, often covering up poor quality frames; this example from Kent has the frame exposed on the lower storey.*

within cob walls continued to be erected and in the northern counties crucks blades, which had fallen from favour on quality housing, were still used throughout the 18th century for small cottages and barns.

By the 19th century there was virtually no new timber framed building in this country, yet in North America and Scandinavia the clearances of vast forests meant that timber was widely available and this form of construction continued and was improved upon with the introduction of modern materials, fixings and mass production. At the end of the Second World War some of these ideas were introduced here and adopted mainly for the public sector housing, partly due to their speed and simplicity of construction and the warmer houses they could create (the bad winters of the late 1940s made this an issue). These houses were built using uniform scantling, lengths of timber cut to the same thickness at sawmills – hence making it cheaper to supply – which were then bolted together on site to make thicker posts and beams.

The walls could be made as a complete unit, known as balloon framing (from the belief that it was as weak as a balloon, although it was the opposite), or as a single storey at a time, called platform framing. This was then covered inside and out by various layers to gave it rigidity and protection from damp before an outer covering of horizontal planks, hanging tiles or a separate brick wall was built (the timber frame is the load-bearing part, the brickwork only weatherproofs the structure). In the 1960s it was common for these to be built between brick cross walls at either end; by the late 1970s, when it was also being adopted by the private sector, the whole house was timber framed and encased in brick. Today a large proportion of new houses are timber framed and all have prefabricated timber trusses holding up the roof. You could be sitting in one right now, unaware that the structure above is being held up by a framework very similar to that of a five hundred year old timber framed cottage!

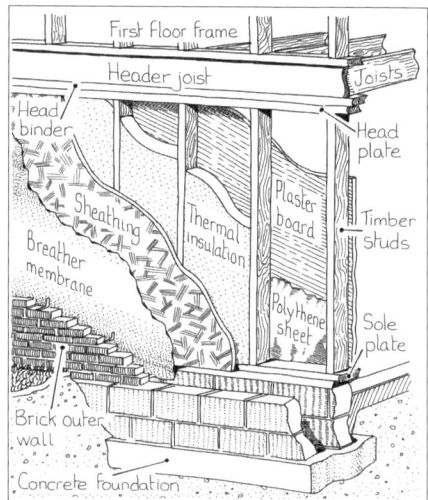

FIG 4.7: *A section through a platform-framed modern house showing the various layers that protect the timbers and the outer brick casing, which weatherproofs it. Although when finished the frame is hidden from view, the fixing of windows to the inner leaf of the wall, the presence of weep holes and air bricks near the base and plasterboard party walls in the loft are clues that it has been built with timber.*

STILL OUT THERE:

FIG 4.8: WEST WYCOMBE, BUCKINGHAMSHIRE: *From the front, this old inn appears a classical 18th-century building but look closely and things are not quite right: the windows are not positioned in a neat proportioned way, they dip towards the right end. The picture below from the rear of the same building shows why; it is a timber framed building onto which a brick façade has been added in the 18th century, so the windows have to reflect the original position and the bowing timbers have affected the bricks and windows.*

FIG 4.9: *Sometimes the timber framed building hidden behind an 18th- or early 19th-century façade is exposed down the side when a neighbouring structure has been removed, as in this case in Shrewsbury.*

FIG 4.10: *It was common from the late 17th century for the old infill to be replaced with brick; the thicker sharp-edged types generally being modern and thinner irregular types earlier. Most windows have also been replaced, as here with square leaded panes in metal frames.*

FIG 4.11: *It was common in the 18th and 19th centuries for smaller houses, like this example from Shropshire, to have the roof raised with a lower pitch using lighter slates or tiles so that a higher upper storey could replace the former limited attic. Shops of all types also extended their fronts to increase space.*

FIG 4.13: *Timber framed farm buildings were common until the 19th century. The gable of this stable at Avoncroft Museum is weatherboarded, a popular covering for farm buildings, often finished in black. Granaries, which appeared in the 18th century due to increased yields (grain was formerly kept in the farmhouse), were frequently timber framed, raised on legs or blocks and limewashed inside.*

FIG 4.12: *Timber framed barns continued to be built throughout the 18th century especially in areas where improved farming techniques had increased yields. They were aisled and crucks structures with opposing central doors, one higher to allow loaded waggons to enter, with the space between used for threshing the corn and the areas either side for storage of crops. The outer panels were filled with wattle or were weatherboarded over, which allowed ventilation to keep the inside dry. In parts of the north, large barns were also built for cattle although these structures are usually encased in stone on the outside, as in this aisled example from Lancashire.*

Georgian and Modern

FIG 4.14: *The famous Rows in Chester are medieval in origin but most of those you see today have Victorian frontages, as in the above example.*

FIG 4.16: *Original timber framed buildings like these on display in Shrewsbury tend to bow and lean (left) while Victorian mock examples are usually strictly horizontal and vertical (right).*

FIG 4.15: PORT SUNLIGHT, WIRRAL: *Many Late Victorian and Edwardian houses used timber frames but usually just a cladding or shallow frontage set above a ground floor of brick or stone.*

FIG 4.17: *Original timbers will usually be rough and cracked (left); those from later mock timber framed buildings will be sharp edged and true (extension on right). The windows on the two sides are later sashes (bottom) and casements (top), while the original mullions with diamond panes have survived in the centre.*

Section II

Timber Framed Buildings in Detail

Chapter 5

The Frame
—— *Posts, Beams and Trusses* ——

FIG 5.1: *Unlike brick and stone structures, traditional timber framed buildings have their load supporting elements visible from the outside; however, this frame is best seen and appreciated from within, especially in some medieval halls and barns as in this crucks example.*

The medieval, Tudor or Stuart carpenter was a very skilled man, responsible for planning, supplying and erecting the whole building. He could not pop down Ye Olde DIY shop, pick up a few planks and use power tools to screw or nail them into place. He had to cut the raw tree trunk, form the joints and make his own pegs with just a handful of basic tools. The carpenter would then assemble the frames, either on site or in his own yard, where after he had carefully marked each joint with matching symbols they were taken to bits and moved the short distance to

45

where they were to be erected. He then had to make sure there was labour at hand to help him carry, lift and fit the pieces into place and form the finished timber superstructure, with the owner only responsible for supplying the refreshments!

Timber

Gathering the necessary timber could not just take place at the drop of a hat but had to be planned around the seasons and the weather. The best time to fell the trees was traditionally in winter, although by the Tudor period the growth of the tanning industry meant it was profitable to do this in spring when the bark, which they could sell to the tanners to cover the cost of felling, was easiest to remove. The most popular tree was oak and most timber framed buildings built before the mid 17th century primarily used this. If it was in short supply then elm might have been used, especially after this date, its timber being extremely good at resisting damp; it was used for piling, even being found intact under medieval bridges! Fir, usually referred to as deal, had been imported on a small scale from the Baltic since medieval times but came into widespread use in the 18th century; being easy to cut it was popular for interior work like stairs and floors in all types of building. Other trees that may have been used include ash, poplar and chestnut, although these tend to be in localities where there was a problem getting oak. Beams from old ships are often quoted as being used in buildings – a few may have been in coastal areas but it is more likely that the mention of ships' timber in documents refers to a particular grade, as we would use 'marine ply' today.

In selecting the tree, the carpenter would look for as straight a trunk as possible for the main beams and posts or a slightly curving one in the case of a crucks frame (in the medieval period the best timber was reserved for the Lord of the Manor and the rights to the rest strictly controlled so there were restrictions about which trees could be used). Once a tree had been felled, the carpenter would carefully choose which parts were used for what job and the best way to cut and divide it up. Cutting the largest pieces could be done

FIG 5.2: *The joints in the main elements of the frame or truss had to be marked after they had been formed and tested so they could be easily identified and fitted together when it was reassembled. This was usually done by simple chiselled or stamped marks (as above) or with Roman numerals on either side of the joint.*

The Frame

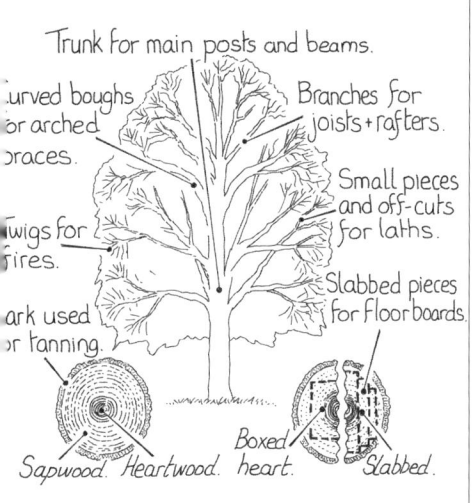

FIG 5.3: *An oak tree with labels highlighting the possible use of its various parts, and sections through it showing how it might be cut into planks. Large trunks used as beams were often called baulks, a name also applied in the north for tie beams and in the 18th century to describe large trunks floated or shipped over from the Baltic. A common medieval term for a beam was 'dormant'; this word over time became 'sleeper' and is still used today for beams under railway tracks and sleeper walls under floors. Bent or curved logs could be split and used for floor joists and common rafters with the flat cut edge facing up. This made maximum use of all the timber but meant each piece was carrying the load on its thinner width. By the 16th century most were set the other way round with the largest dimension resisting the load and hence curved pieces could not be used.*

over a rectangular pit with a long saw pulled back and forward between someone above and below, or by splitting them with wedges. Cross saws and axes were used to cut and trim the timber to size while an adze, or later planes, made a smooth surface (the concave gouges associated with antique beams are supposed to represent marks made by the curved blade of the adze).

Joints

The joints between beams and posts were formed with tenon saws and chisels, with augers or wimbles (see Fig

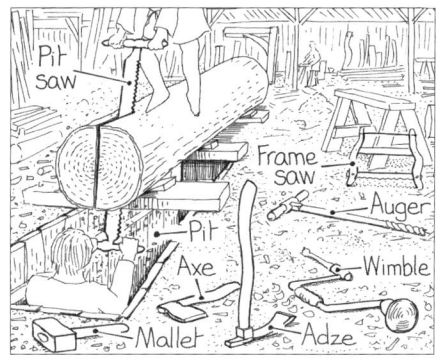

FIG 5.4: *A medieval carpenter's yard showing some of the tools needed to make a timber framed building. The saw pit is being used to cut a tree trunk, with the saw pulled between a man on top and a less fortunate one down below. An adze – an axe with curved blade at a right angle to the handle – was used to trim wood. The curved gouges are taken today to imply antiquity, but in the right hands an adze could produce a smooth surface. Wimbles and augers were used to make holes.*

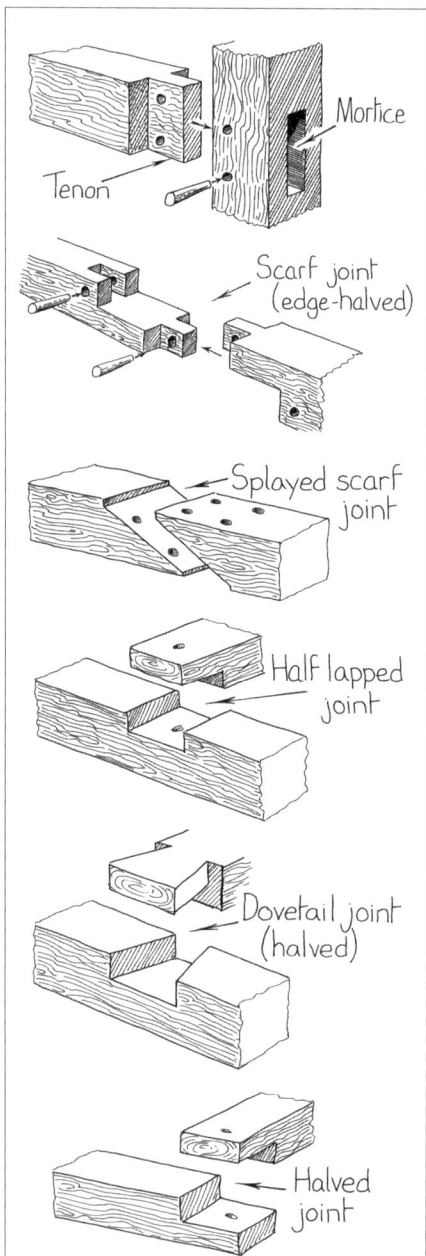

FIG 5.5: *A selection of some of the most common joints used in timber framed buildings. From top left they are a mortice and tenon joint, edge half scarf joint, a splayed scarf joint, a half lapped joint, a dovetail joint, and a halved joint (in a corner). Above is a tie beam lap dovetail assembly, which combined mortice and tenons, lap and dovetail joints to secure the junction between the wall post, wall plate and tie beam.*

5.4) to make the holes for the wooden pegs. The type of joint made by the carpenter depended on the size and position of the pieces it was connecting and the direction of force they were likely to come under (whether they would be pulled in tension or pushed together in compression). The most widely used was the mortice and tenon joint, with a rectangular tongue at the end of one piece fitting into a similar shaped slot in the side of the other and a slightly tapered round wooden peg rammed into a hole that had been drilled through both to hold it firm (the holes were slightly off line so the peg was held tight). As it was often hard to get long, straight timbers, a scarf joint

The Frame

was used to link two pieces together in a line in its simplest variant, with two sloping edges or halved ends pegged together, while in others more elaborate arrangements using these basic forms were developed. Where two lesser timbers pass over each other, a simple lap joint was used, especially in earlier houses; however, if one part was under tension then a dovetail joint to stop it being pulled away from the other could be best. A more complex variation, which combines these two along with a mortice and tenon, is the tie beam lap dovetail assembly, which linked the post and tie beam to the wall plate and was widely used up until the 19th century.

The frame

The type of frame composed from these timbers and joints, as mentioned in the previous chapters, varied depending upon period and location. Crucks frames had their principal blades formed from two halves of a slightly curving trunk, which were squared off and then leant up against each other to

FIG 5.6: *Foundations of timber framed houses were rarely substantial, with usually just the top soil removed to create a level, firm surface. It is likely that the sill plate was temporarily raised up a foot or two on blocks. Then, when the building was complete, the gap below was filled in with stone and brick in mortar. In Yorkshire, the vertical posts rested upon large pad stones or stylobates with the sill plates tenoned into the sides of them a couple of feet above the ground (see also Fig 2.14).*

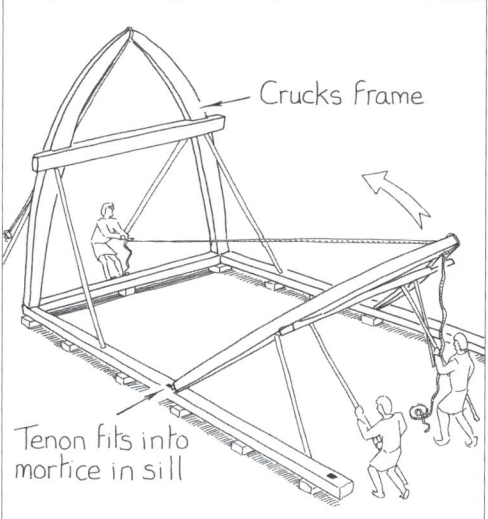

FIG 5.7: *Crucks frames were reared into position, possibly as shown above, with their lower ends fitting into sockets in the sill and the upper sections raised up to the vertical by ropes and poles. The principal longitudinal pieces, the wall plate and purlins, were then fitted between the bays formed by the series of crucks frames. The rearing could be a social event, like harvesting, when the owner would supply refreshments.*

form a rough triangle. A tie beam across the middle or a collar higher up linked these pieces to form an 'A' shaped frame with its length carrying on beyond the crucks or having short spurs to meet wall plates or rafters. Vertical wall posts could then be added to form the long external face of the building and other timbers filled the gap under the frame at the ends. Because the crucks did most of the load-bearing the wall posts did not have to be as substantial as in other types of building (see Fig 5.1). In some large buildings the blades ended short of the top and were linked by a collar with a different form of frame above; these base crucks could also be lifted off the ground and set into a stone wall. In later buildings, raised crucks were occasionally used with short blades only going down as far as a tie beam, with what in effect appears to be a roof truss resting upon stone side walls.

Post and truss buildings had load-bearing wall posts linked by a tie beam, with principal rafters carrying the side and ridge purlins completing each cross frame, which were laid out in a line along the length of the building. Box framed buildings, which are similar in appearance, did not have the rafters forming part of the frame, but had posts and beams making up the side

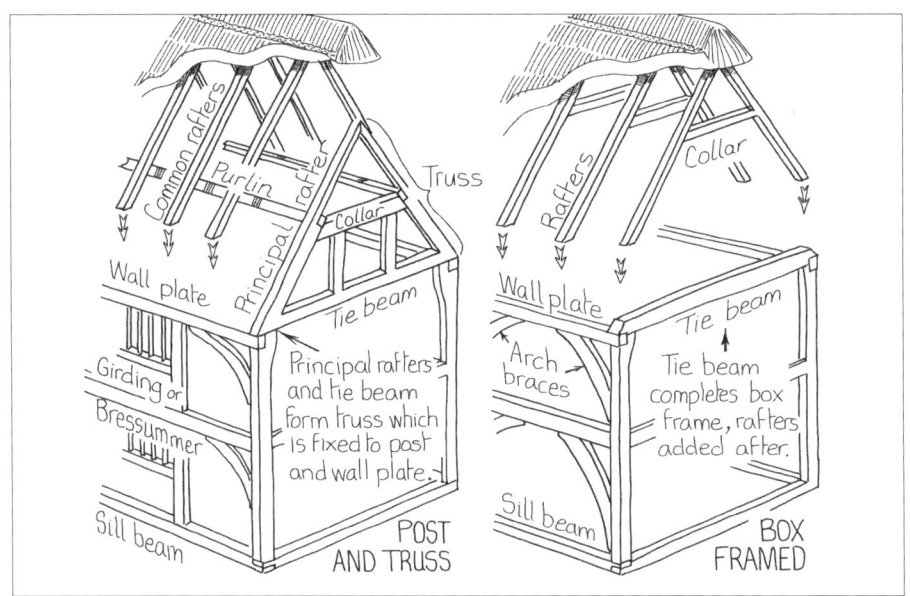

FIG 5.8: *Labelled drawing of a post and truss building (left) where the principal rafters are part of the cross wall with thinner common rafters between and a box framed building (right) in which similar sized rafters are separate from the structure below.*

The Frame

FIG 5.9: *At the entrance to some medieval halls a single large arched opening was formed between two short walls called speres. This impressive timber assembly is known as a spere truss.*

and formed the arcade (the large posts dividing the central part and the side sections); the horizontal beam they supported was called the arcade plate. These were linked to the lower outer wall posts, which held up the horizontal aisle plate. In some, additional long braces running from the lower part of these up through the frame and fixed into the timbers they passed (passing brace) were used. The arcade posts transferred most of the weight of the roof onto the ground, often via seemingly precarious stone pillars. These verticals proved convenient in barns, where aisled types remained popular into the 18th century (see Fig 4.12), but they caused obstructions in halls and are usually only found in 13th and 14th century examples.

Roof structure

Supporting the heavy roof covering and giving it sufficient strength to cope with the extra weight of it being covered in snow (there was a mini ice age from

and end walls with the roof structure added afterwards as a separate element.

All of these types of structure would be vulnerable to wind pressure or movement, which could cause the frames to topple over, so braces were always included (although they might be hidden behind an outer decorative finish). A straight or slightly curved piece was tenoned in between post and bressummer or wall plate to form a rigid triangle (a tension brace ran down from the post to a horizontal beam).

Aisled halls and barns enabled a larger area to be spanned compared with most other types. It was essentially a post and truss structure with lean-to aisles up the sides but all under a single roof (see Fig 2.8). The load-bearing vertical posts were inside the building

FIG 5.10: GREAT COXWELL BARN, OXFORDSHIRE (EH): *An aisled barn with the arcade posts resting upon stone columns.*

1400–1700 so winters could be harsh) was the most important role of the frame. In crucks buildings this was done by the blades either directly having the purlins fixed on them or having spurs to transfer this weight from a rafter. In the other types of timber framed buildings a long line of matching rafters or a series of trusses transferred the load down onto vertical wall posts with some form of tie beam or braced collar holding the walls against the outward force from the roof (see Fig 1.2).

The simplest form of roof was a single framed type, which had a row of rafters pitched either side, with the thin laths fixed on top to which the covering was attached. This was sufficient for short spans but required more support on larger buildings so a collar was fitted between the rafters. However, with just the laths stopping each pair from toppling over, some longitudinal stability was required so a horizontal crown plate could be added through the middle of the roof, fixed underneath each collar and supported by crown posts resting on the tie beams at the end of each bay. There were usually curved braces fixed under the collar or crown plate and into the post, which itself could be carved with a moulded caps and base. These rather over elaborate roofs are impressive structures in the finest medieval buildings, mainly in the east and south of the country.

Double framed roofs had longitudinal purlins carrying most of the weight of the structure above, supported by principal rafters, which formed part of a truss at the end of each bay. In areas where crown posts had been popular, the purlins tend to be held between a collar or strut and the underside of the rafter, which is usually reduced in thickness above this point, these clasped purlin roofs becoming dominant from the 16th century (see Figs 3.9 and 5.12). An alternative method was to fix the ends of the purlins into the sides of the principal rafters, either in a continuous line, butt purlins, or staggered so the tenons did not clash with the next one along, tenoned purlins (see Fig 5.12). In areas of the North, West and in the Midlands, where crucks frames had been dominant, trenched purlin roofs with thick principal rafters and the purlins cut into the top side of them were popular from the 16th century.

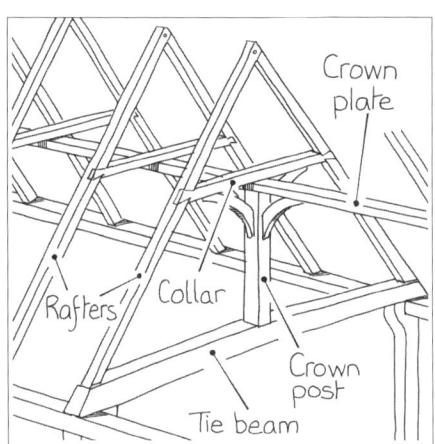

FIG 5.11: *Single framed roofs had no purlins, just rafters with no supports on short spans, collars on wider ones and a crown plate resting upon posts on the largest and finest medieval examples, as shown above.*

The Frame

FIG 5.12: *A form of double framed roof with trenched purlins; this was common in the 15th and 16th century in the Midlands and the north of the country. The braces help resist the pressure upon the end of the building from the wind. Other methods for holding the purlins are shown below.*

FIG 5.13: *An arched brace roof with cusped wind braces making a dramatic effect.*

These trusses usually had a pair of struts, a collar or both running up from the tie beam to support the rafter under the point where the purlin was trenched into it.

On larger spans the tie beam would tend to sag in the middle under its own weight. In northern counties the king post truss (see Fig 2.13) was a common type used throughout the medieval and later periods; carpenters probably intended its thick central post to hold up the ridge but in practice it helped stop the tie beam bending in the middle. This effective arrangement became popular across the country in 18th and 19th century buildings. In some trusses the tie beam was excluded, with a collar higher up supported by arched braces (see Fig 2.9) and with the principal rafters cut around the wall plate at the bottom. These were usually found in the highland zone where they were often fitted in the middle of a hall so as not to obstruct the open space. Another solution used in the finest and widest medieval halls was the hammer beam truss (see Fig 2.9), which in effect cut the central section of the tie beam out and had the remaining ends (the hammer beams) supported by arched braces rising from the wall below.

Joists and jetties

The framework for any floors that were inserted between the outer walls was composed of joists and bridging beams, which before the 17th century were usually exposed in the ceiling below. The joists were fixed to the girding plate or rested upon a ledge along its back and then ran across the short width to a

Timber Framed Buildings Explained

FIG 5.14: *Most medieval and Tudor ceilings had the timbers supporting the floor above exposed in the room below. In all but the smallest houses a bridging beam (left in the above picture) was a substantial timber that supported the joists halfway across the span. In this example there is also a diagonal dragon beam, which was used when a jetty ran around both walls (see Fig 5.16).*

houses moulded. Medieval joists were laid on their longer flat side, not the strongest arrangement but it meant that bent pieces could be used. In Tudor and Stuart houses, where timbers were generally straighter, they were laid out in the conventional manner.

In the later medieval period, jetties became a popular feature of buildings, especially those in urban areas. They were constructed by extending the floor joists over the wall or jetty plate of the frame below by a foot or two and then either having the lower beam of the wall above resting on top of them or jointed onto the ends. This latter solution was the more decorative as it covered the ends of the joists and the beam was usually carved with a moulding running down its length (see Fig 3.7). When a large beam running down the centre of the ceiling. This bridging beam was often the most substantial piece of timber in the building and its underside was usually chamfered or in the finest

FIG 5.15: *The floor joists in a timber framed building could either rest upon a ledge pegged to the rear of the wall studs (left) or rest on the top edge of a horizontal girding (right).*

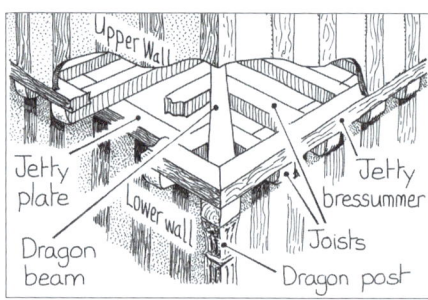

FIG 5.16: *A view of a corner of a building with a jetty continuing down both sides and the wall cut away to show a common arrangement of timbers to support the floor above. As the joists had to have their ends pointing out, a diagonal dragon beam was required into which to fix them. The exposed end of this rested upon a dragon post, which was often carved with decorative patterns or figures (see Fig 5.17).*

The Frame

FIG 5.17: *There were a number of ways in which the ends of the joists could be finished. In some of the finest buildings the jetty bressummer was fixed onto the ends of the joists and its outer face was moulded (left). The most common arrangement, especially in early examples, was to have the ends of the joists exposed (centre) while in some cases a coving was applied below (right). Note in these three views the plain and decorated dragon posts in the corners.*

---

jetty was continued down one or both sides of the building a more complicated arrangement of joists was required, with diagonal dragon beams supporting the joists (see Figs 5.14 and 5.16). Although this slight extension of upper floors increased the room space, the main reason for fitting them was more likely to be the potent status symbol from the impressive tiered effect of one or more jetties, and the opportunity it gave for decoration.

Later changes

The main structure when well built from good quality timber could last hundreds of years, yet even in the finest examples some parts of the frame would need repair or replacing, especially those lower down, which were prone to damp. This could be done in the case of the main posts by drilling a hole through them and running a rod or needle into it with the ends jacked up so a lower part could be cut out and a new section fitted in (these holes can sometimes still be found in posts, although they could have been used for the original rearing). Just as the frame had been pieced together, it was possible to take it apart and move it; before the 19th century this would rarely be any great distance, due to the weight of the timbers and the patchy quality of transport, for instance it may have been done when an old hall was rebuilt as a barn in a nearby farm. This could also happen when the owner built a more up to date house on a new site with the old building being downgraded for agricultural storage. It was also common for old village farmhouses to be split up into cottages when a parish was enclosed and new buildings built out in the middle of the fields.

FIG 5.18: *It was common for later extensions to be added to the main structure, especially wings, stair turrets and porches. In this case, the old outside wall is still visible between the two parts and any doorway fitted between them will show signs that it was cut through, as in this example where the vertical studs have been cut off (see their bases in the sill) to allow access into a porch, which was added after this house was completed.*

FIG 5.19: *It is common to see notches on the face of timbers inside and outside a building. These were made as a key for plaster, which was applied over the frame to disguise it, usually in the late 17th to early 19th century. This covering has commonly been removed in the 20th century as exposed timbers became fashionable, leaving the pitted surface as the only sign that it was once hidden.*

FIG 5.20: *Many timber framed buildings have had new roofs fitted with a lower pitch due to the lighter weight of slates, which became available from the late 18th century. Some used it to make the upper storey higher; others, as in this truncated farmhouse, simply replaced the former steeper thatch roof.*

CHAPTER 6

The Infill
Wattle and Daub
and Roof Coverings

FIG 6.1: *The infill between the timbers varied with fashion and local availability of material. Wattle and daub (right) was the most widely used but various other types can still be found (left) as well as forms of cladding that covered the whole frame (centre rear).*

Once the main structural frame had been assembled, the gaps between the beams and posts would have to be filled and the roof covered. Horizontal rails and vertical studs were added as the frame was assembled (although they could be moved or taken out at a later date) to form the spaces for the panels. In medieval examples these were generally large but by the Tudor period close set vertical studs and smaller square frames were fitted to the better

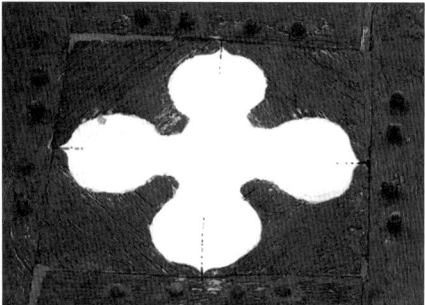

FIG 6.2: *Decorative framing was composed of ornamental panels, either formed from timber pieces pegged into a square panel (top) or complete wooden panels inserted in four parts to form a pattern like a quatrefoil (bottom).*

woven branches, the wattle, and covered inside and out with a plaster-like substance, the daub. Firstly staves, straight sticks usually of oak, were inserted into holes, with the other end slid into a groove to create vertical supports set around half a foot apart. Then branches of hazel or oak were woven horizontally between the uprights (in some parts of East Anglia the supports were set horizontally and the sticks were just tied to them).

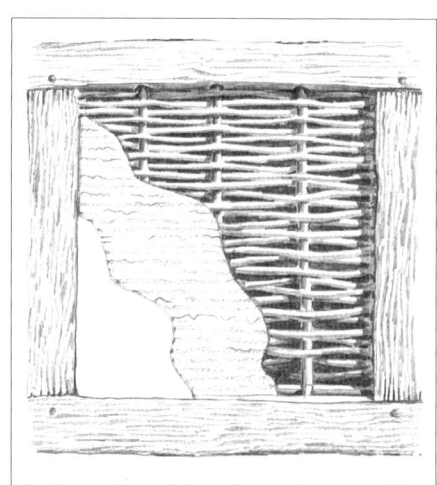

FIG 6.3: *One type of wattle and daub panel with a cut out to show the vertical staves, which fitted into holes at the top and slid into a groove at the bottom. After the weave was fitted the daub was applied and left with a rough surface as a key for the final coat of plaster. This was made from limestone burnt in a kiln to produce quicklime, then mixed with water (shalking) and left to mature to form a lime putty, which was mixed with sand and animal hair to make the final smooth coat.*

quality buildings. During the late 16th and early 17th century this latter arrangement could be further elaborated upon with the insertion of small straight or carved pieces, which were fixed to the frame or slotted in grooves to create decorative patterns in the panels.

Wattle and daub

The most common infill used on timber framed buildings was made from

The Infill

Next the daub was made, principally from clay, straw and dung (although other ingredients were sometimes added), mixed with water and left until it had almost dried. As the daub would shrink as it dried, it was left until the last moment to be applied to the inside and outside of the wattle in pliable lumps worked firmly into the weave. The surface was usually scoured or pitted to give a good key to a final coat of lime plaster, which was applied when the daub had dried (the surface was moistened to help it bond), leaving the panel flush or slightly recessed from the front edge of the frame (where the infill protrudes today this is the result of later work).

Limewash and painting

Once the panels had dried they would usually be covered in a limewash to weatherproof them and fill in any small gaps that draughts could get through, a process that was probably repeated every couple of years or so. This was a mix of lime putty and water, which would be applied over the surface and would dry as off white, sometimes with a yellow or pink tinge depending on the ingredients. Because of the high alkaline content of limewash it was good at protecting the timber from pests and also gave it a small degree of fireproofing.

It is not known for certain how the complete outside wall was originally finished and it was probably down to the individual or local practice as to the chosen scheme. In some, just the panels were limewashed and the oak frame left to weather to a silvery grey, especially on better quality timber framed buildings like those with close studding and decorative panels that the owner would want to show off. In others, the whole outer surface was washed over (even stone buildings were sometimes limewashed over to protect them from the effects of water penetration, hence the White Tower in the Tower of London).

The medieval and Tudor world was full of colour and it is also likely that many timber framed buildings would have been painted with russet red, yellow ochre, pinks and other earthy tones, either picking out the frame or covering the panels, or the complete front of the building. These paints were limited by the ingredients available in

FIG 6.4: *Some timber framed houses may have been limewashed or painted over the whole surface, as in this example. Many would have bold colours on the exterior; black and white, which we are familiar with today, would have been rare and only became standard practice in the 19th century.*

the locality and could include substances like bull's blood, soot and animals' urine to create the desired pigment. The black and white scheme that is so characteristic of timber framed buildings today is a fairly modern creation; bright whites were only available from the late 19th century and although blackening of timbers may have happened from an early date in areas like Cheshire, it was generally a Victorian fashion, when tar and later bitumen became widely available.

Other infills

There were alternatives to fill the panels, especially in the later periods. In barns, where a degree of ventilation was required to keep contents dry, split oak wattles were woven between the vertical staves and left un-daubed so air could pass between them. In some, grooves were set in the edges of the frame and horizontal boards or decorative wooden panels fitted into them. With close studding, where the gaps were narrow, a vertical weave, thin oak laths, broken tiles or stone

FIG 6.5: *Other forms of infill that can be found in timber frames. Oak boarding and split wattles are usually left unpainted and are often found on agricultural buildings. Brick, shown here laid in a herringbone pattern, was a popular infill in more recent centuries although some original examples can be found in the east of the country. The narrow gap between close set studs could have been filled with thin wooden strips (laths), stones, tiles or staves, which were then plastered over.*

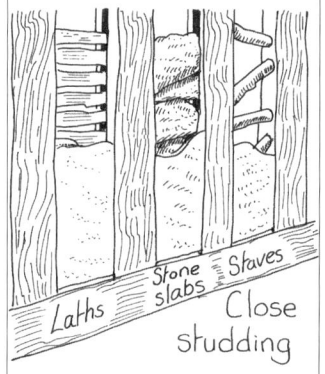
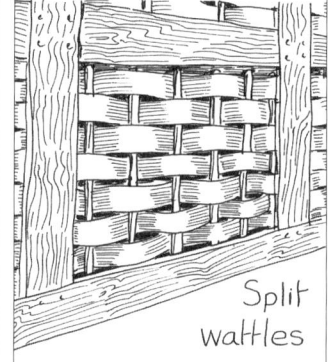

The Infill

slabs would be slotted in and then plastered over.

Today, brick is often found filling panels in timber framed buildings, sometimes fitted in neat courses, other times in diagonal herringbone patterns. These tend to be later infills, replacing worn wattle and daub panels in the 18th or 19th century. There are some, however, that are original fillings, mainly in the eastern and southern counties in the Tudor and Stuart period, with distinctive thin and irregular bricks. Unfortunately, as old bricks could have been inserted at a later date you can only be sure whether they were the first filling used if they are removed and the frame inspected for a groove at the bottom and holes at the top, to show where wattles were originally fitted or not. It is also worth noting that bricks are not a good material for this role; they are a poor insulator, they can hold in moisture affecting the timber and they are heavy, which can put strain on a frame that was intended to support much lighter wattle and daub.

Later coverings

As timber framing became unfashionable from the mid 17th century, many owners covered up the façade of their buildings to make them appear more up to date, and add some extra protection against the elements and better insulation. In the past, the plaster applied to the panels was sometimes carried on over the frame to make a more fire resistant finish, which could have raised patterns built up upon it called pargeting (it was used from an early date in parts of East Anglia but most that you see today is a late Victorian or more recent creation). In later examples, horizontal laths were fixed across the old frame and the layers built up upon these so the finished surface could be scoured to imitate stonework and disguise its unfashionable construction.

Weatherboarding is characteristic of the South-East and some coastal regions, where it was used from an early date to provide protection from the elements. It gained more general popularity from the late 18th century,

FIG 6.6: *Three types of cladding that could be fitted to buildings when originally built or as later coverings to hide and protect the timber frame beneath.*

FIG 6.7: *Examples of pargeting where a pattern was either raised up on top of the plaster, cut out of it or pressed in. It is characteristic of houses in East Anglia but most of what is seen today dates from the 19th or 20th centuries.*

mathematical tiles, which were designed so their exposed faces would imitate bricks. Their hidden lip was fixed to boards across the frame, then they were mortared in, leaving a rectangular section which can be difficult to tell from a complete brick building. In some situations the whole façade was covered by a new brick or stone wall tied to the original frame, which was still visible down the sides, rear or under an archway. This was very common in urban areas and along turnpike roads where a fashionable frontage was important for business.

Roofing materials

The type of roof covering used depended upon the local materials available. The structure below was built at a pitch steep enough to suit its weight and ability to shed rainwater, so heavy types like thatch and stone slabs when machine-cut timber made it a cheap option to cover old frames or to hide poor quality structures, and was common on farm buildings.

Hanging tiles or slates were another option; these were suspended from laths fixed to the frame and overlapping each other, as on the roof. A better quality finish could be achieved with

FIG 6.8: *Thatching was the most widely used roof covering in the medieval period but fell from favour in urban areas from the 16th century due to the fire risk.*

were best fixed at around 45°–50° while some clay tiles or slates could be as shallow as 25°–30°. If the covering was set at too shallow a pitch there would be a tendency for the walls to be pushed outwards and for rain to penetrate under the gaps between the layers. Sometimes mortar was applied between tiles and slates to reduce this latter effect, although this blocks ventilation into the loft and causes problems with damp on timbers.

Thatch was widely used on all buildings until from the 13th century it fell from favour in urban areas as fires forced many authorities to ban it, although how strictly this was applied probably varied until regulations in the late 17th century were adhered to. In the country it remained in use up until the late 19th century and then has been revived in our modern and more affluent times. The best type to use was water reeds, which could last for at least half a century; wheat straw, which was more readily available, would need changing every twenty years or so. This life span was also shortened depending upon the climate and in the damper western and northern regions it would need replacing more regularly.

Clay tiles, which had been widely used by the Romans, came back into use from the 13th century, usually in the eastern counties where they were first imported before the skills to make them here were established. Pantiles with their wavy profile were common in the east and some coastal regions while smaller flat tiles came into more general use in towns and cities. Holes would be formed in their upper edges and small pegs inserted, which held them on the thin oak laths that ran horizontally along the rafters. In areas where there were sedimentary rocks (composed of layers of sediment, which could be easily split along these beds) slabs or slates could be used. They would be sorted out into rough sizes on site by the

FIG 6.9: *Clay tiles (left) could be pegged or had moulded lips, which hung off laths running across the rafters (centre left). Stone slates (centre right) had small holes knocked through for pegs to be inserted and hung over the laths in a similar way (right).*

roofer and the smallest ones were put on the ridge and the largest, heavier ones down by the eaves where the walls could best support them. Holes were carefully knocked out at the top and they were pegged over the laths in a similar way to tiles. Tiles made from oak – called shingles – were also used in the past although modern types tend to be made from cedar, which can be thinner, lighter and hence set at a lower pitch.

All of these coverings need replacing at some time and although it is ideal to use the same material that had been originally intended by the carpenter, many have been changed, largely due to costs and regulations. As times got hard in the countryside towards the end of the 19th century and skills were lost, thatch was often replaced by corrugated iron sheets, a light and efficient but noisy and unsightly covering. From the late 18th century, thin Welsh slates became more widely available. They would last longer than thatch and could be set at a lower pitch so many cottages had their front walls raised to create a full height upper storey as a result.

FIG 6.10: CHURCH LOFT, WEST WYCOMBE, BUCKINGHAMSHIRE: *A late 15th-century building with later brick infill, laid out in horizontal courses, and a tiled roof.*

CHAPTER 7

The Fittings
— Windows, Doors and Floors —

FIG 7.1: *One of the most distinctive features of a timber framed house is its windows, ranging from the simple open mullion to the elaborately carved projecting types. However, these and other details would have been changed to suit fashions so this chapter explains what might have been originally fitted.*

Unlike a modern house, where a brick shell can have a whole range of different style fittings inserted, many of the features of a timber framed building were part of the frame itself. Although they are dealt with here as separate sections, windows, door frames and ceilings were usually fitted as the structure was initially assembled. The finer details of these parts also varied upon period, region and even the individual carpenter and are an important area of study beyond the scope of this book (see *Period House Fixtures and Fittings 1300–1900* by Linda Hall).

Windows

Medieval timber framed buildings originally had windows that were simply a gap in the frame with vertical wooden mullions inserted within. These were set into diamond-shaped sockets top and bottom so the sharp edge of the mullion faced out (ones set square tend to be later replacements or replicas). At this date glass was expensive and limited in availability so most houses had wooden shutters, which slid horizontally, or occasionally vertically, in grooves on the inside of the frame (external hinged shutters are a later fashion). In more basic housing, oiled cloth may have been hung instead, but whatever the solution, the building was open to the elements or very dark if not! In most cases the exterior face of the window was plain, although the edge of the opening could be chamfered or moulded. In the finest buildings, carved pieces could be inserted between the top of the mullions or across the whole head to create the effect of pointed Gothic windows.

By the Tudor period projecting windows could be found on the finest buildings. These more elaborate fittings were a separate frame, which was tenoned onto the timber around a gap in the wall so they would protrude out for either just the thickness of the frame or, more commonly, by sufficient depth for a small window to be squeezed into

FIG 7.2: *A mullion window in its original form, with sliding internal shutters just visible behind. The diagonally fitted mullions could have had glazing added between them at a later date or would have been filled in, leaving just an outline in the wall.*

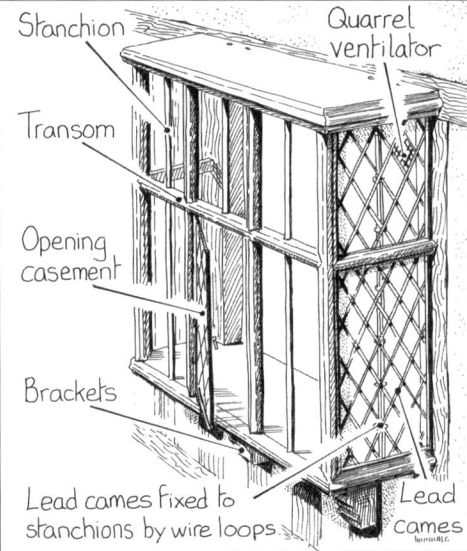

FIG 7.3: *A projecting window with the glass removed from the front face to expose its frame and parts. An air flow through the sealed window could have come from a hinged casement in one of the lights or a vent in a quarrel.*

the return. The parts were carved with mouldings and usually had small brackets below, which were often decorated. A horizontal bar, called a transom, was fitted in many of these in order to give support to the panels of glass that were now fitted.

Glass, like bricks and tiles, was a product introduced here by the Romans but for which the manufacturing skills were lost after they left. It was imported from the Continent in the Middle Ages, with home produced glass fitted into the finest buildings by the 15th century. However, it was not until the late 16th century that it became widely available for most buildings. At this date only small pieces could be produced, cut into diamond shapes and held in lead cames to make up a small panel, which was inserted either into a mullion or projecting window. Because the pressure from the wind could blow out the delicate glass, a vertical metal or wooden rod – called a stanchion – was fitted with wire loops fixed to the lead to give it support. Ventilation still had to be provided so either one of the panes was hinged so it could be opened (a casement) or one of the quarrels (an individual piece of glass) was left out and a small metal vent inserted in its place.

Windows, especially those on the main façade, have usually been subject to change more than once and most timber framed buildings will have later wooden casement or sash windows. It is usually down the side or rear that older mullion windows can be found, with the gaps either glazed or filled in.

FIG 7.4: *The glass used in the 16th century was spun from the end of a long rod when molten until it formed a large, nearly flat disc. It was then cooled and cut up into pieces with the bull's-eye piece in the centre usually thrown back in to be reused (it is a modern fashion for this piece to be fitted in windows to create an antique effect). Original glass that still survives from this period can have a rippled surface and tiny air bubbles within, as in the above example.*

Doors

Doors on timber framed buildings were hinged to close flat onto the inside of the door frame and were not recessed within it, as was typical from around the mid 17th century. The surround for the entrance was part of the frame of the building and not a separate door case, as would be fitted in a stone or brick structure. The jambs (the sides of the opening) were often chamfered or had a simple moulding running down their edge, which ended short of the ground at a decorative piece called a stop. The door head along the top was straight or had a profile, from a simple triangle to a double 'S' shaped ogee arch, the most elaborate having Gothic tracery inserted in the corners to form a distinct pointed arch. These sometimes have the name of the owner or carpenter along with a date carved in them, although as with any inscription upon buildings they can relate to an extension or updating of the structure and not the original build.

The door in its simplest form was composed of vertical planks held together by horizontal battens along the rear. Metal strap hinges were fixed along the front with their looped ends hooked over a pintle, a vertical metal pin bracketed off the frame, so that it always opened inwards. A few medieval doors survive on churches and other important buildings; most original ones that can be found on timber framed structures date from the 16th century onwards. These earliest examples tend to have three or four broad planks, often of irregular width and with a

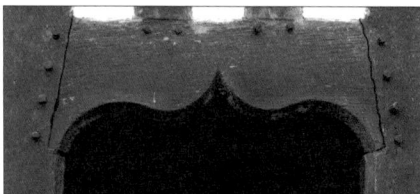

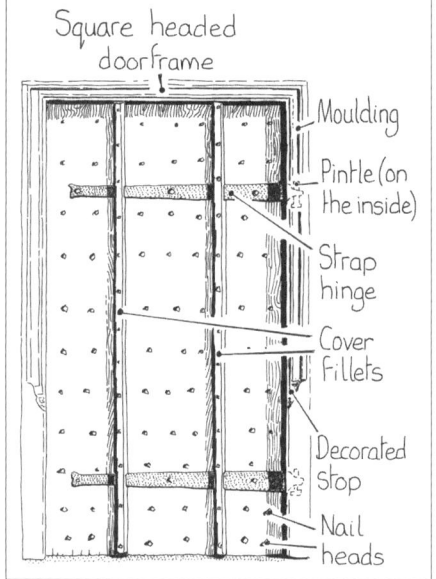

FIG 7.5: *Door heads were horizontal timber pieces pegged into the frame and could have simple triangular (top) or ogee arch (centre) profiles to their lower edge or could be carved into arches with Gothic decoration above (bottom). Shallow arches tend to be later in date.*

FIG 7.6: *Example of a plank and batten door formed from three irregular planks, with vertical fillets covering the gaps and the nails used to fix the battens behind covering the whole for a decorative effect. The edge of the surrounding frame has been moulded and this finishes at a carved detail called a stop.*

The Fittings

rough and worn finish; later replica ones usually have narrower and straighter pieces. These plank and batten doors could be further elaborated with the addition of vertical strips covering the joints and framing the edge, which blocked gaps that could let draughts in and made a more impressive face. Some doors also had horizontal strips added, which imitated a panelled door, but true panelled doors composed of a frame with panels inserted are rare on timber framed buildings and only came into widespread use in the later 17th century.

Stairs

Most medieval houses had a principal room, which was opened to the rafters; it was only in the finest buildings that a second floor could be found, usually in a private wing. As a result, stairs were rare and those that were fitted tended to be simple, either tucked away in a

FIG 7.7: *The earliest stairs may have been little more than a pair of steep bearers (the side beams) onto which were pegged the blocks which formed the steps. Sometimes their underside was cut to rest flat on top of the bearers (the blocks therefore have a triangular profile from the side) as in the right-hand one in this picture, or they were fitted into the inner edge as in the left-hand bearer here.*

FIG 7.8: *A winder stair (top) and closed well with a cut-away of its central frame (bottom).*

passage or up against an end wall in the hall. Some were no more than ladders, others had triangular profiled blocks forming the treads, which were held between two bearers.

As floors were inserted and new houses built with two levels during the 16th century so staircases became a standard feature, although they were usually tightly packed into a square planned space, often to the side of the chimney with doors top and bottom. The wedge-shaped treads could be fixed to the door frame, built up upon a solid mass that housed an oven in the room below, or were supported by a separate vertical post called a newel.

In the largest buildings a broader set of stairs were fitted, often within a separate stair turret with separate treads and risers fitted around a newel post, or into a hollow timber framed central block, which was panelled off. By the 17th century this latter structure was removed and open well staircases with carved or turned balusters and decorated newel posts became a feature for display, although they were still found in a separate enclosed space within a tower or at one end of a hall.

Floors and ceilings

In most timber framed houses these were one and the same thing; the joists and beams that supported the floorboards above were open to view in the room below. The earliest examples sometimes have the boards set in recesses along the edge of each joist, so its upper surface becomes part of the finished floor, this rather elaborate system being replaced by the more conventional laying of the boards at right angles on top of the joists by the late medieval period. The boards tend to be of uneven width at this date; the widest were put in the middle and the narrower around the edges of the room. They were nailed onto the timbers below, in the finest work with the heads carefully hidden from view. Only much later did narrower tongue and groove boards become available, the earlier versions having grooves down both edges with a separate tongue inserted into them when they were installed.

The ceilings in most timber framed buildings would have joists fitted into a larger central bridging beam, which usually had a chamfer or carved moulding along its bottom edges. In important rooms these timbers could be arranged to create a decorative effect, with beams forming a central square section or chequerboard patterns, and with carved wooden discs, called bosses,

FIG 7.9: *Large floorboards from a 17th-century house with later thinner ones (top left) used to repair a section.*

over the junctions between them. Some even had boards fitted between or over the joists, with painted decoration. By the turn of the 17th century it was becoming fashionable to have a plaster ceiling, at this date in only the finer buildings and not becoming a widespread practice until the 18th century. These were applied onto laths fixed to the underside of beams and joists, which would be of the same height (where an exposed timber ceiling has this today it is usually a sign that it was intended to take a plaster ceiling, which has been removed in modern times).

Ground floors could be timber in important rooms, or when there was a basement or cellar, but usually they would have been little more than beaten earth. Substances like bull's blood could have been mixed in to bind the surface and rushes, which would be replaced monthly, sprinkled on top to collect dirt. Stone flags were reserved for better quality houses and brickwork was usually limited to fireplaces; it was only from the 17th century that these became more common further down the social ladder; many cottages still had the former crude type of floor up into the late 19th century.

Panelling and painting

Internal walls could be formed from square framing with wattle and daub panels, in effect just thinner versions of the exterior. Some had vertical planks slotted into posts, or in later versions overlapping each other to create an in and out wall. The finished surface was often painted with bright and colourful scenes and patterns running over plaster and wood alike, many of which have been uncovered in recent times and fragments of which can be seen on display today.

In the finest cases, wooden panelling was fitted across, insulating the room and creating an air of quality. The earliest examples of panelling occur in screens – movable or permanent walls built across the ends of medieval halls, with doorways to gain access from the screens passage. By the late 15th century, timber framework with panels carved in linenfold patterns became fashionable in the finest rooms, with moulding along the top and sides of each panel and an easy to dust chamfer along the bottom (where this arrangement is different it can indicate that the panelling has been re-sited from somewhere else or is a replica). In the late 16th and early 17th century,

FIG 7.10: *A more elaborate ceiling with the junction of the bridging or ceiling beams covered by a boss and with the joists arranged to form a geometric pattern.*

Timber Framed Buildings Explained

FIG 7.11: *Linenfold panelling (left) and plain square panelling (right). Note the flat chamfer on the dusty bottom edge for ease of cleaning*

earliest halls and many cottages through into the 17th century had nothing more than an opening in the apex of the roof for smoke from the fire to escape, usually with a cap or louvre above to keep the rain out. This was improved upon in many later buildings by fitting either a smoke bay – a partition above head height at one end of the hall, which would trap the fumes – or a smoke hood – a timber framed square funnel in a corner, which did much the same.

The development of chimneys with narrow flues, which drew the smoke up smaller, square panels were fitted, often with a wooden frieze along the top edge; the bottom always rested directly upon the floor. If a skirting is fitted it will be a later addition or again implies that this is not original work.

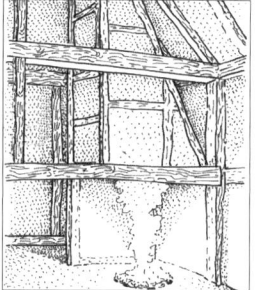 

FIG 7.12: *In many medieval halls the fire was not centrally placed but was confined to a corner with either a wedge-shaped timber smoke hood above it (left) or a panelled off end of the room above head height, called a smoke bay (right). They were daubed inside to reduce the fire risk and where they do survive today it is often because a later brick flue and chimney were built within them. When looking at a chimney within a timber framed building, the way that the beams around it either vanish into the brickwork or seem designed to fit around it can tell the expert eye whether it was built in an old smoke bay or whether it was an original fitting.*

Chimneys and fireplaces

For any Tudor or Stuart gentleman about to sit down for the first time in his new house, the greatest change he would instantly appreciate over his older open plan home would have been the fireplace. Rooms with lower ceilings, panelled walls and a large fire with a good draw, thanks to the chimney, would have been so much warmer than before, a bit like going to the Mediterranean for the first time after holidaying in Skegness! The

The Fittings

FIG 7.13: *Chimneys from the 16th and early 17th century varied from stocky ones originally in the centre of a house (the left example is stone but now has a later brick extension on top) to elaborate, tall brick stacks (right).*

as the wind passed across the top, was a revelation to the design of interiors, creating a smoke free atmosphere and enabling floors to be inserted and private chambers fitted above. Their importance can be determined by the elaborate tall, twisting and decorated stacks that are such a distinctive feature of Tudor and Elizabethan manor houses, and those who were still building in timber could not wait to follow suit. They were typically fitted in the centre of new houses or up against an outside wall or passageway (see Chapter 3) and had large open inglenook fireplaces, those in a main living room or kitchen with a bread oven to one side.

FIG.7.14: *A roaring fire, low beams and candlelight casting flickering shadows over rustic oak furniture completes the idyllic view of a snug English timber framed dwelling, as potent an image in this late Tudor farmhouse as it is still is today for many country pubs and luxury houses.*

Further Information

Hopefully this book has explained the background to these fascinating types of building; if you wish to take your study further or want to know about a particular house then the following tips and books are well worth investigating.

The *Buildings of England* series, originally by Nikolaus Pevsner, are a county-by-county guide to architecture and the property you might be interested in may have been covered in this. Internet search engines are worth a try – because of the age of these buildings there may have already been studies carried out upon them. The local library may hold a copy of the *Victoria County History* of the area (not every county is covered yet), which is a rich source of documentary evidence. There may also be a copy of the surveys carried out when a property was listed as being of architectural importance, which most timber framed buildings should be on age alone. A physical study and photographing of details such as joints – even better if you can get safe access to the roof structure in the loft – are invaluable and the information gathered can then be shown or sent to local experts in the field.

It is unlikely that one source will have all the answers and a combination of documentary evidence, matching styles with others in the locality of a known date, and existing studies will be required to better understand the building in question. There is, however, one method available that can accurately date a beam or post, in some cases down to the time of year the tree it came from was felled! Dendrochronology is the study of tree rings, which vary in width during wet or dry years, and by painstakingly noting the patterns formed, like a barcode, a record for timbers in a local area can be created. Core samples can then be taken from a timber and can be compared against this list to find a matching pattern, and hence the date, when the tree was cut down. If this has already been carried out on a building, it should be remembered that the dating only applies to the beam or post from which the sample was taken. Although this would be from a major piece, which it is fair to assume would be a part of the original structure, the timber could have been reused from an older property or might be a repair and hence have a younger date. Despite this caution, dendrochronology has revolutionised the study and dating of timber framed buildings.

Places to Visit

There is a wide range of timber framed buildings to visit, many maintained by the National Trust, English Heritage or local authorities and just a few notable examples which are regularly open to the public are listed here.

SHIBDEN HALL, Lister's Road, Halifax HX3 6XG. 01422 352246 Grid ref: SE106257. 15th century open hall.

LOWER BROCKHAMPTON, Greenfields, Bringsty, nr Bromyard, Herefordshire WR6 5TB. 01885 488099 brockhampton@nationaltrust.org.uk. 14th century manor house.

RUFFORD OLD HALL, Ormskirk, Southport, Lancs L40 1SG. 01704 821254 ruffordoldhall@nationaltrust.org.uk. c1480 screen and hammer beam roof.

LITTLE MORETON HALL, Congleton, Cheshire CW12 4SD. 01260 272018 littlemoretonhall@nationaltrust.org. Probably the finest and most complete large timber framed house.

LONG CRENDON COURT HOUSE, Long Crendon, nr Aylesbury, Bucks HP18 9AN. 01280 822850 Grid ref: SP698091.

MERCHANT ADVENTURERS' HALL, York YO1 9XD. 01904 654818. 14th century guild hall.

BARLEY HALL, York YO1 8AR. 01904 615505 www.barleyhall.org.uk.

BOSCOBEL HOUSE, Staffs, (nr Wolverhampton) ST19 9AR. 01902 850244. Grid ref: SJ838082.

SPEKE HALL, The Walk, Liverpool L24 1XD. 0844 800 4799 spekehall@nationaltrust.org.uk. Large 16th century manor house.

ANNE OF CLEVES HOUSE, Lewes, East Sussex BN7 1JA. 01273 474610 www.sussexpast.co.uk/anneofcleves

FORD GREEN HALL, Smallthorne, Stoke on Trent ST6 1NG. 01782 233195

To really appreciate a timber framed structure, old barns should be visited where there are no obstructions to block your view.

EAST RIDDLESDEN HALL, Bradford Road, Keighley, West Yorks BD20 5EL. 16th century barn with king post.

GREAT COXWELL BARN, Great Coxwell, Faringdon, Oxon SN7 7LZ. 01793 762209

BREDON TITHE BARN, Bredon, nr Tewkesbury, Worcs. 01684 855300

LEIGH COURT BARN, 5 miles west of Worcester, Grid ref: SO 783 535 Largest crucks structure in Britain.

Timber Framed Buildings Explained

BRADFORD ON AVON TITHE BARN, Bradford-on-Avon, Grid ref: ST823604. 14th century monastic barn with crucks frame roof.

PRIOR'S HALL BARN, Widdington (nr Newport), Essex, Grid ref: TL537318. Aisled barn with crown post roof.

COURT LODGE, Agricultural Museum, Brook, Kent TN25 5PS. 01304 824969. 14th century aisled barn.

SOUTHCHURCH HALL MUSEUM, Southchurch Hall Close, Southend, Essex. 01702 467671. 14th century hall.

There are also some towns and villages which are rich in timber framed buildings. **Chester**, **York**, **Ludlow**, **Warwick**, and **Shrewsbury** are of note. Spon Street in **Coventry** has an outstanding collection of restored timber framed shops, and there is a smaller scale version in **Tewkesbury** with a museum (Little Museum, 45 Church St GL20 5SN. 01684 297174). The best villages which are a must to visit are **Lavenham**, Suffolk and **Weobley**, Herefordshire, many photos in this book come from these two exceptionally well preserved sites.

There are also a few museums of note which I would recommend visiting to see timber framed buildings in their original form:

AVONCROFT MUSEUM OF HISTORIC BUILDINGS, Stoke Heath, Bromsgrove, Worcs B60 4JR. 01527 831363/ 831886 www.avoncroft.org.uk

WEALD AND DOWNLAND OPEN AIR MUSEUM, Town Lane, Singleton, West Sussex PO18 0EU. 01243 811363 www.wealddown.co.uk

RYEDALE FOLK MUSEUM, Hutton le Hole, York YO62 6UA. 01751 417367 info@ryedalefolkmuseum.co.uk

Spon Street, Coventry.

GLOSSARY

ASLAR:	Smooth, squared stone masonry with fine joints.
AXIAL:	A feature located, or a plan laid out, along the axis of a house.
BALUSTER:	Plain or decorated post supporting the stair rail.
BALUSTRADE:	A row of decorated uprights (balusters) with a rail along the top.
BARGEBOARD:	External vertical boards that protect the ends of the sloping roof on a gable and were often decorated (many are Victorian in date).
BAULK:	A regional term for a large timber beam.
BAY:	A vertical division of a house between trusses. Usually reflected on the façade by a column of windows.
BAY WINDOW:	A window projecting from the façade of a house up a single or number of storeys and usually resting on the ground.
BEAM:	A large horizontal timber.
BONDING:	The way bricks are laid in a wall with the different patterns formed by alternative arrangements of headers (the short ends) and stretchers (the long side).
BOW WINDOW:	A vertical projection (bay) of semicircular or segmental plan.
BRESSUMMER:	A term that can refer to a number of horizontal beams but especially the one on the bottom of the upper wall of a jettied building.
BRIDGING BEAM:	A large beam running down the centre of the ceiling, into which the joists are fixed. It usually has chamfered or moulded lower edges.
BURGAGE:	A unit of land in an urban borough, usually taking the form of a narrow strip, with a house or shop at the end facing the street.
CAMES:	The soft metal strips in which the small panes of glass are fitted in a leaded light window.
CAPITAL:	The decorated top of a Classical column.
CASEMENT:	A window that is hinged along the side.
CHIMNEYPIECE:	An internal fireplace surround.
CORBEL:	A stone or timber bracket built into a wall and usually supporting the base of a roof truss.
CORNICE:	A moulding that runs around the top of an external or internal wall.
COVING:	A large concave moulding that covers the joint between the top of a wall and ceiling or under a projecting window.
CRUCKS:	Two slightly bent large timbers set resting upon each other to make an arched support to hold the roof. The individual timbers are known as crucks blades.
DORMER:	An upright window set in the angle of the roof and casting light into the attic rooms.
DRAGON BEAM/POST:	The diagonal beam and supporting post where jetties down the side and front of a building meet.
EAVES:	The section of the roof timbers under the tiles or slates where they project over the wall, often with a fascia board that supports the guttering.
FAÇADE:	The main vertical face of the house.
FENESTRATION:	The arrangement of windows in the façade of a house.
FIELDED:	The raised central part of a panel.
FINIAL:	An ornamental piece on top of a railing or the end of the roof ridge.
FLUTING:	The vertical concave grooves running up a column or pilaster.
FRIEZE:	The middle section of the entablature, in this context referring to the section of the wall between the picture rail and cornice.
GABLE:	The pointed upper section of wall at the end of a pitched roof.
GIRDING BEAM:	Can be a heavy beam carrying binders in a large floor or a beam fitted into the wall, onto which the joists rest.
GLAZING BARS:	The internal divisions of a window, which support the panes.
GUILLOCHE:	A decorative pattern made from two twisted bands forming circles between.
HALF TIMBERING:	Another popular term for timber framed construction. In some cases used to refer to a building with a stone or brick lower storey and a timber framed upper.
HEARTH:	The stone or brick base of a fireplace.
JAMBS:	The sides of an opening for a door or window.

Timber Framed Buildings Explained

JETTY:	An upper floor that projects out and is supported by extending out the floor joists.
JOISTS:	Horizontal beams that support the floorboards and are usually exposed in the room below.
LATH:	A thin strip of wood pinned to posts or joists to support a covering of plaster.
LINTEL:	A flat beam that is fitted above a door or window to take the load of the wall above.
MOULDING:	A decorative strip of wood, stone or plaster with a shaped profile.
MULLION:	A vertical bar dividing a window.
NEWEL:	The principal vertical post in a set of stairs.
NOGGING:	A solid infill usually of brickwork with a timber frame.
ORIEL:	A large projecting window supported from the wall on an upper storey.
PARAPET:	The top section of wall that continues above the sloping end of the roof.
PARGETING:	A raised pattern formed from plaster on an external wall (popular originally in the east of England).
PEDIMENT:	A low-pitched triangular feature supported by columns or pilasters above a Classically styled door or window in this context.
PILASTER:	A flat Classical column fixed to a wall or fireplace and projecting slightly from it.
PITCH:	The angle by which a roof slopes. A plain sloping roof of two sides is called a pitched roof.
PLINTH:	The low stone or brick base around a timber framed building.
POST:	A large vertical load-bearing timber.
PURLIN:	A horizontal timber beam that runs along the pitch of a roof.
QUARREL:	A diamond-shaped pane of glass set into cames to make a leaded light window.
QUOIN:	The corner stones at the junction of stone or brick walls.
RAFTERS:	The diagonal beams forming the triangular framework that supports the roof. Principal rafters form the upper part of trusses.
RAIL:	A lesser horizontal timber usually infilling between main posts and beams.
RENDER:	A protective covering for a wall.
REVEAL:	The sides (jambs) of a recessed window or door opening.
SASH WINDOW:	A window of two separate sashes, which slide vertically (or horizontally on smaller Yorkshire sash windows).
SCANTLING:	Lightweight timbers used in building. Uniform scantlings are all of one standard dimension of cross section.
SHALKING:	The chemical process that takes place when burnt lime is mixed with water to produce lime putty which was used in mortar and limewash.
SILL (or CILL):	The horizontal timber beam at the bottom of the wall, usually resting upon a brick or stone plinth.
SKIRTING:	The protective strip of wood at the base of a wall.
SOLAR:	A private chamber usually on an upper floor behind the upper end of the hall.
STANCHION:	An upright post or support.
STRAPWORK:	Flat bands that form decorative patterns, from the 1580s–1620s.
STRING COURSE:	A horizontal band running across a façade and usually projecting.
STUD:	A lesser vertical timber usually infilling between main posts and beams.
TENON:	The projection which fits into the matching hole (mortice) in a mortice and tenon joint. Also the name of a type of saw used to cut it.
TRACERY:	The ribs that divide the top of a window and are formed into patterns.
TRANSOM:	A horizontal bar in a window.
TRUSS:	A triangular frame of timber beams supporting the roof.
VERNACULAR:	Buildings made from local materials in styles and method of construction passed down within a distinct area, as opposed to architect designed structures made from mass produced materials.
VOUSSOIR:	The wedged-shaped stones or bricks that make up an arch.
WAINSCOT:	Timber lining of internal walls or panelling.
WALL PLATE:	The main horizontal timber that runs along the top of the wall and under the eaves.

Index

A
Avoncroft Museum of Historic Buildings, Worcs: 23, 42, 76

B
Barns: 12, 17, 18, 23, 42, 75–76
Box framing: 18–19, 20, 31, 50–51

C
Chester: 43, 76
Chimneys: 27–29, 72–73
Churches: 12, 14, 18, 21, 68
Close studding: 19, 21, 31, 32, 60
Crucks framing: 19, 23, 24, 45, 46, 49–50

D
Decorative framing: 32–33, 58
Doors: 67–68

E
East Anglia: 17, 19, 21

F
Floors: 9, 28, 29, 53–54, 70–71

Ford Green Hall, Staffs: 34, 75

G
Glass: 30, 67
Great Coxwell Barn, Oxon: 51, 75
Greensted, Essex: 12

J
Jetty: 6, 25, 29–30, 54–55
Joints: 9, 45, 47–49

K
Kent 17
Kings Lynn, Norfolk: 33

L
Lavenham: 33, 76
Leek: 11, 36
Leigh Court Barn, Worcs: 23, 75
Limewash: 59
Little Moreton Hall, Cheshire: 8, 35, 75
Ludlow, Shropshire: 22, 34, 76

M
Marton, Cheshire: 21
Midhurst, Sussex: 38

N
Nantwich, Cheshire: 34
Newcastle upon Tyne: 35

P
Panelling: 71–72
Pargeting: 61–62
Port Sunlight, The Wirral: 43
Post and Truss: 18–19, 31, 50–51

R
Roofs: 8, 9, 10, 11, 18–19, 20, 22, 31–32, 51–53, 62–64

S
Square framing: 32–33, 57
Shops: 14, 22, 76
Shrewsbury, Salop: 23, 34, 41, 43, 76
Stairs: 69–70
Stokesay castle, Shropshire: 35
Suffolk: 20

T
Tewkesbury, Glos: 22, 76
Timber: 45–47
Trusses: 10, 18, 30, 31, 39, 45, 50

Index

W

Waltham St Lawrence, Berks: 13
Wattle and Daub: 33, 57–59, 71
Weald and Downland Museum, West Sussex: 22, 76
Wealden houses: 13, 22, 24
Weatherboard: 39, 61–62
Weobley, Herefordshire: 24, 76
West Wycombe, Bucks: 41, 64
Windows: 6, 27, 43, 65–67

Y

York/Yorkshire: 21, 22, 25